"Every biblical and Reform[...] preparation for his people[...] it be a weekly or monthly [...] new title of Log College Press. God's people will find it profitable in [...] spiritual lives. I recommend it."

> -- David Myers, Retired Pastor and Teacher in the Presbyterian Church of America

"I was pro-Janeway right from the Preface—his remarks about loquacious ministers who don't give saints silence to do business with their Lord at the supper were 'spot on.' His meditations show how fascinated he is—and wants us to be—with 'the infinite and complex person of the Redeemer.' I found his 'post-communion' meditations on thanksgiving, obligation, watchfulness, and joy among the most gripping and helpful. Janeway seems to assume that Jesus gave us the Supper as our means of renewal—and, if so, why do we need scads of 'revival' meetings and retreats and seminars and conferences?"

> -- Dale Ralph Davis, Former Pastor in the Presbyterian Church in America and Professor of Old Testament at Reformed Theological Seminary in Jackson, Mississippi

"In his meditations, Jacob Jones Janeway offers extraordinary insights into one of God's gloriously ordinary means of grace. This little book will richly bless you by awakening your soul's senses to the thrilling privilege and amazing love on display at the Lord's table."

> -- Jim McCarthy, Senior Pastor, First Presbyterian Church in Hattiesburg, Mississippi

MEDITATIONS ON THE LORD'S SUPPER

Jacob Jones Janeway

LOG COLLEGE PRESS

www.logcollegepress.com

Meditations on the Lord's Supper
By Jacob Jones Janeway

Log College Press
92 Cotton Wood Dr.
Madison, MS 39110
www.logcollegepress.com

Page and cover design by Emmalyne Beck

Printed in the USA by Color House Graphics,
Grand Rapids, Michigan

ISBN: 978-1-948102-39-1 (Paperback)

ISBN: 978-1-948102-40-7 (ePub)

ISBN: 978-1-948102-41-4 (Mobi)

CONTENTS

FOREWORD

Jacob Jones Janeway was born in the city of New York, late in the year 1774, on November 20th. The eldest child of George and Effie Ten Eyck Janeway, he was raised in a Christian home, his parents being members of the Reformed Dutch Church. Subsequent to the Battle of Long Island in August of 1776, British troops took possession of New York City, and young Jacob's parents were forced to take him and flee the city, not returning until 1783. So from the age of nine, Jacob's education took place in the city of New York, up to and including college, entering Columbia College at the age of fifteen and graduating there in 1794 with high standing among his peers.

Jacob's mother had long hoped that he would enter the ministry, yet he was caught up in the temptations of worldliness in his college years, came close to becoming a skeptic, and for a time felt directed to a medical career. But a sermon delivered by an otherwise unnamed pastor began to work upon his heart, and it was at this point that his father's pastor, the celebrated Dr. John H. Livingston, counseled him to cast all upon the righteousness of Christ.

Being at the time a member of the Reformed Dutch Church, he was first licensed by the Classis of New York in 1798. Then in 1799, he was ordained by the Presbytery of Philadelphia (PCUSA) as colleague pastor with the Rev. Dr. Ashbel Green, of the Second Presbyterian Church, Philadelphia. That service of ordination took place in the Old Arch Street Church on Thursday, June 13th, and was notable in that Janeway was ordained along with four other men—John Blair Linn, William and John E. Latta, and Buckley Carl. Janeway noted in his diary,

On this auspicious day I was solemnly set apart to the work of the ministry of the Lord Jesus. In the presence of God, of his holy angels, and of men, my most solemn vows were made. May the Lord God and Savior, the Great Head of the Church, endue my soul with abundant fortitude for the all-important work, and bless me with great success. I give thanks, oh God, for thy presence on the affecting occasion.[1]

A further note in his diary soon after his ordination serves to give added evidence to the depth and fervor of his piety and love of the Lord:

Through the week God has favored me with composure and serenity of mind. My thoughts have been collected. But alas! I have to lament the corruptions of my soul. Oh! What unbelief, what pride, what coldness of affection; how hard to lift the soul to God by fervent breathings of heart. O Lord, I beseech thee to bestow liberally on me of the influences of the Holy Spirit. Prepare me, Lord, for thy sovereign pleasure. Sanctify me, oh God![2]

Dr. Green and young Janeway labored together with uninterrupted harmony in this important charge for thirteen years, until such time as Dr. Green was transferred to the Presidency at Princeton College in 1812. Dr. Green refers in his diary to Dr. Janeway in the following terms:

We were colleagues for thirteen years. It was with him that I had an explicit understanding that we should remember each other in our daily prayers, and treat each other's character as if it were his own. The consequences were most happy. We labored and loved as brethren during the whole period of our collegiate connection, and an untroubled and ardent attachment has existed between us to the

---

1. *Memoir of the Rev. Jacob J. Janeway, D.D.* Philadelphia: Presbyterian Board of Publication, 1861, p. 32.

2. Ibid, p. 32.

present hour. I still pray for him daily in my private devotions.[3]

After the resignation of Dr. Green in 1812, the Rev. Dr. Thomas H. Skinner was chosen colleague of Dr. Janeway; and when Dr. Skinner resigned in 1816, Dr. Janeway remained sole pastor of the large and flourishing church, which then stood on Arch street.

A dedicated and careful churchman, it was during these years that he compiled a Digest from the records of the General Assembly (1820). In 1818, Dr. Janeway was also elected Moderator of the General Assembly.

In 1828, Dr. Janeway was appointed by the General Assembly to serve as Professor of Theology in the Western Theological Seminary at Alleghenytown, which was then commencing operations. For reasons somewhat unclear, but primarily having to with an "uncertainty" in the school's property title, Dr. Janeway resigned in the following year. We consider that a sacrificial step on his part, rising out of his high ethical standards.

In 1830, he accepted the call of the First Reformed Dutch Church in New Brunswick, New Jersey, one of the largest congregations in the United States at that time, and continued as pastor there for about two years, only resigning the charge on account of his health and advancing years.

In 1833, he was elected Vice President of Rutgers College, which office he held until his resignation in 1839. Among the last of his courses taught there was a class on evidences of Christianity. Lectures prepared for that course in 1838 were later incorporated into one of his major works, *The Internal Evidence of the Holy Bible* (1845). In 1838, Dr. Janeway's final act of service in the Reformed Dutch Church was to serve as President of their General Synod.

In 1839, he re-united himself to the Presbyterian Church, and served in various important offices, in the extension of the Redeemer's kingdom.

---

3. Ibid, p. 22.

Such was his service as a member of the Executive Committee of the Board of Foreign Missions, as President of the Board of Domestic Missions, as President of the Directors of the Theological Seminary at Princeton, and as Trustee of the College of New Jersey, that he was widely noted for his wise counsel, his punctuality, and his general influence and example, so contributing to the well-being of the Church and her ministries. He was notably a man of high character, with strong traits of perseverance and attention to duty.

The book you hold in your hand is a master class in the meaning and importance of the Lord's Supper. There is rich meat here for your soul, served up in convenient portions. Keep this book by your bedside or chair and read a chapter before the Supper is to be celebrated; or you might even read it both before and after the service for better benefit. You will be rewarded.

WAYNE SPARKMAN
DIRECTOR, PCA HISTORICAL CENTER
ST. LOUIS, MISSOURI

Dr. Janeway wrote and published a number of works, among which are the following:

1812
Letters Explaining the Abrahamic Covenant. 302 p.

1818
An Essay on the Inability of Sinners. 24 p.

1820
Janeway, J.J., William Neill & Ezra S. Ely, *A Digest, compiled from the records*

of the General Assembly. 391 p.

1827
Letters on the Atonement. 242 p.

1828
Inaugural Address, upon installation as professor of theology in the Western Theological Seminary. 15 p.

1829
Janeway, J.J., *A sermon, delivered at the ordination of Nicholas Murray, A.M. to the gospel ministry.* 32 p.

Papers read...on resigning his office as Professor of Theology in the Western Theological Seminary. 24 p.

1835
The Scriptural Doctrine of the Atonement Illustrated and Defended. 28 p.

1836
The Duty of the Presbyterian Church. A discourse, delivered before the General Assembly. 52 p.

1838
An Exposition of a Portion of the Epistle to the Romans: in the form of questions and answers. 135 p.

1842
An Exposition of the Epistle to the Hebrews: in the form of questions and answers. 144 p.

1844
Unlawful Marriage. 215 p.

1845
The Internal Evidence of the Holy Bible. 287 p.

1848
The Communicant's Manual. 264 p.

1852
A Family Piece: or, A Memoir of Mrs. Martha Gray Janeway. [Rev. Janeway's deceased wife]. 207 p.

1853
Hope for the Jews. 246 p.

1856
Antidote to the Poison of Popery in the writings and conduct of Professors Nevin & Schaff. 335 p.

1856
*Hope for my country, showing the divinity of Jesus Christ and his care over his church...*64 p.

PREFACE

The Author, in preparing for the Holy Supper, has, for many years, been in the habit of conducting his private unwritten meditations, in a manner somewhat like the form adopted in these meditations. Recently it occurred, that a series of written Meditations on appropriate topics, might assist communicants who are unskillful in the art of private meditation. Relying, therefore, upon Divine aid, and humbly hoping for the blessing of the great Head of the Church, on his attempt to edify some of the members, he undertook the work.

He has written *nineteen* meditations, to be used before the communion; *one*, at the Holy Supper; and nine, after the communion. To all, except one, he has appended short prayers.

To read devoutly a Meditation will require from *eight* to *ten* minutes, and a prayer, from *two* to *three*.

If notice for the Supper be given two weeks before the administration, there will be ample time for reading over these Meditations and Prayers. If only a week should intervene, they might be read by allowing more time for devotional exercises, morning and evening; or a selection may be made, so as to suit the time.

After using this little book for a while, many may find themselves enabled to intersperse new thoughts, in reading over these Meditations; just as a person may add reflections, when perusing a chapter, or part of a chapter in the Holy Bible.

It is not the wish of the Author, that any should confine themselves to the prayers appended to these Meditations. He has written them to direct the reader's attention to those parts of the Meditations, which furnish matter for praise, thanksgiving, and prayer; and which he may incorporate with any address he feels disposed to offer unto God, after devoutly reading them.

Between such a use of these prayers four times a year, and confinement to set forms of prayers every Sabbath, and every day of the year, there is no analogy.

The writer invites the attention of his brethren in the ministry to the *twentieth* Meditation, designed to direct the exercises of communicants, when seated at the Lord's table. It will, he presumes, be admitted, that communicants have a very important duty there to perform, and that their minds ought to be occupied with thoughts like those suggested in that Meditation. This being granted, will it not follow, that they should be allowed time sufficient for each one to follow the train of thought to which he feels inclined; to make the confession of sins, to present the petitions, and to offer the thanksgivings, suited to his own case? But if, at the administration of the elements, the minister is constantly speaking, how can communicants perform that peculiar duty, which is to be transacted between his own soul and his Redeemer, as he ought? Must not such incessant speaking sadly break in upon his secret devotions?

When the writer is seated at the holy table, and the elements are being distributed, he feels a wish to be left alone to his own meditations; and he endeavors to shut his ears to any address by the minister; because it appears to him then so unseasonable. No doubt many communicants feel as he does; but they may not be able to abstract their minds from the address of the speaker.

But, it will be said, "Do not communicants need thoughts to be thrown out to assist their meditations?" Granted; they need assistance: and let it be proffered to them at the proper time. Cannot a minister say all that needs be said, before he distributes the bread? And if afterwards he wish to utter a striking thought, or to give an appropriate direction, can he not do it in few words, when he distributes the cup?

That communicants ought to be left to their own meditations and exercises, while the elements are being distributed, the Author has, for many years, been so fully convinced, that to address them, at such a time with continued remarks, he would feel to be an unwarrantable intrusion on their private devotions.

With all due respect to the judgment of his brethren in the ministry, he submits these few thoughts on this subject to their serious consideration. He will only add, that he thinks the general adoption of such a plan would render communion seasons more profitable to communicants.

NEW BRUNSWICK
JANUARY, 1848

Meditations on the Lord's Supper

Meditation 1

Precious Ordinance

Again the administration of the Lord's supper has been announced; and on the appointed day, it will be my privilege and that of other disciples of our Lord, to take our seats at his table. Invaluable ordinance! How powerful its influence in sustaining Christian character and deportment! The announcement of it has often found professing Christians slumbering and declining, if not backsliding. Aroused by it, in attending to the duties and meditations which preparation for it demands, they have discovered their slumbering and declension; and been by grace enabled to awake from sleep, and to recover what they had lost.

How precious this ordinance on various accounts! The consideration of its *origin* should endear it to our hearts. It did not take its rise from human wisdom. It is no appointment of man. No man, whatever may be his station and authority has a right to ordain a religious rite; nor has any assembly of men, whether civil or ecclesiastical, such a right. The exercise of such a right would be an invasion of the authority of the Lord Jesus Christ, the great Head of the Church. He alone has a right to prescribe her laws, and to ordain her rites. Were the supper a human appointment, it would be *mere will worship*; and, in partaking of it, we might justly apprehend his rebuke, instead of expecting his approbation.

The great Lawgiver and Head of the Church instituted this ordinance. He made the appointment in circumstances of peculiar endearment. The same night in which he was betrayed, when he had a full view of his approaching sufferings, then his love appointed this supper, designed for the edification and comfort of his disciples, till the end of time. In such circumstances he took bread and wine, as memorials of his broken body and shed blood; and commanded them to be used as such, in remembrance of his sufferings for us, and his love to us. Three Evangelists, and the apostle Paul, have certified us of these facts (Matthew 26:26-30; Mark 14:22-25; Luke 22:19, 20; 1 Corinthians 11:23-33).

This ordinance was first observed by the apostles of our Lord in a large upper room in Jerusalem (Mark 14:15); then by the Church in that city, after the Redeemer's resurrection; and subsequently by the Church, wherever she was found in various parts of the world, in all succeeding ages; and now it is observed by the Church in these ends of the earth; and it will be observed by the Church till the end of the world. Let me then remember this great fact, of which not a doubt should exist, that this supper was appointed by the authority of Jesus Christ; and let me partake of it in obedience to his authority, and thus render it an act of acceptable worship.

How precious this ordinance, when we consider who are the invited guests, and by whose presence the supper will be graced and honored! Whom shall I see at the table of my Lord? The rich, the great, the nobles, the princes, and kings of the earth? Oh! No. Seldom have such been found to obey the Savior's dying command. They prefer sitting at tables, which wealth and pomp delight to provide, spread with costly viands, that gratify and pamper their bodily appetites; and slight a feast designed to meet the wants of an immortal mind, and nourish its spiritual life, and prepare it for heavenly happiness. There shall I meet the poor, the unlearned, the unknown. Yet let me lift the veil that conceals them, and look at them with the eye of faith; and whom do I see? How changed! They are the disciples of Christ, the ransomed of the Lord, the saints of God, his children, the sons and daughters of the Almighty, the heirs of heaven, the expectants of crowns and kingdoms there. What a privilege! What an honor to sit with them at the same table of our common Lord!

Nor is the Lord absent. He is indeed in heaven. His glorified body is there, far removed from mortal sight. But, in his divine nature, Jesus is everywhere; and he will not fail to meet, with his gracious presence, his disciples, when, in obedience to his dying command, they gather around his table, to feed upon the spiritual repast his love has prepared for them. Compared with such a feast, partaken of by such guests, and graced with the presence and enriched with the smiles of the King of kings and Lord of lords, what is the most sumptuous entertainment that was ever prepared by earthly riches, for the display of human grandeur and magnificence!

How precious too this supper, when its spiritual nature is considered! Heresy will have it, that the words of the institution are to be understood *literally*; that, in the supper, we eat the *real* body and drink the *real* blood of our Redeemer; and that the elements are really changed into his body and blood. What absurdity! When the Savior said, "I am the door;" "I am the vine;" are we to understand him as meaning, that he was *really a door*, and *really a vine*? Heresy itself is compelled to assign a figurative meaning to some words in the institution. She does not contend we are to drink the *cup* and not the *wine*, when the cup is given; nor that the cup is *really* the *New Testament*, and not a sign and seal of it. "It is the spirit," said Jesus, "that quickeneth; the flesh profiteth nothing: the words that I speak unto you, they are spirit, and they are life" (John 6:53-56, 63).

The feast is not designed to satisfy our bodily appetites. It is a spiritual feast, intended to nourish our spiritual life, and strengthen all the faculties and graces of that life. A small portion of bread and wine, used as symbols of the broken body and shed blood of our Lord, is given to us, that we may feed on his body and blood, not *carnally* and *corporally*, but *spiritually* and *mystically*, by faith. We are to receive, and eat, and drink the elements, to signify that, as we live by eating and drinking appropriate food, so we live spiritually by feeding by faith on the spiritual food, which he furnishes for the life of our souls; or, in other words, that we are willing to accept that spiritual and eternal life he has purchased by his sufferings and death, and to depend on him for its preservation, increase here, and final expansion in the world to come. Such is the nature of this blessed feast.

The supper of our Lord is precious also on account of the covenant engagements it seals. "This cup is the New Testament in my blood, which is shed for you" (Luke 22:20). The covenant of grace was ratified and sealed by the blood of the great Mediator, and all its blessings were made sure to all for whom he undertook to satisfy divine justice; and the cup or wine, the symbol of this blood, seals the New Testament or covenant in this ordinance. Here I am invited to renew my covenant engagements with God. Here I am allowed the great privilege of taking God the Father, the Son and the Holy Ghost to be my covenant God; the Father to be my reconciled father and covenanted portion, through Christ; the Son to be my Savior, friend, master and Lord; and the Holy Ghost to be my guide and teacher, my sanctifier and comforter; and to give myself up to God as his servant and child; to Christ as his disciple and follower, and to the Holy Ghost as his temple, forever. The elements are seals to this covenant, for both parties. I seal my engagements to God; and God seals his promises to me.

Amazing transaction! What astonishing condescension and grace on the part of God! And how should I admire and adore him for such condescension and grace!

Is this the feast I am invited to partake of? So heavenly in its origin, and instituted in circumstances so interesting; its guests so noble and dignified; its nature so spiritual, so nourishing to my spiritual life, and so strengthening to every grace and virtue; and the transactions to which it invites so wonderful and sublime? How joyfully ought I then to embrace every opportunity of supping and communing with my blessed Lord!

For such an ordinance doubtless a corresponding preparation is required. By solemn meditation on suitable topics, by self-examination, by renewing my covenant engagements, by the exercise of repentance and faith, and by earnest and importunate prayer, let me then, endeavor to prepare for a believing and profitable communion season.

Prayer

Blessed Redeemer, I praise thee for the institution of thy holy supper. I thank thee that, in circumstances so distressing, when thou hadst before thee all that thou wast about to suffer in the garden, in the palace of the high priest, in the hall of Pilate, and on the cross, thou didst not forget thy disciples. Then thou didst provide this memorial of thy love, this feast for the welfare, comfort, and edification of thy Church, to the end of time.

May I highly prize this ordinance, and rightly appreciate the high honor conferred on me, and the precious privilege granted to me, in being permitted to commune with thy people, and with thee, my Lord and Master! May my heart rejoice at every announcement that this precious supper will be again administered in the church of which I am a member!

Surely it becomes me to make a suitable preparation for taking my seat at a table covered with so rich a feast. Grant, O Lord, that I may come, having on the wedding garment, that I may meet with thy approbation, my King and my God. Incline my heart to meditate seriously and solemnly on all those interesting topics that will claim my attention; to examine myself; to recollect my sins and renew my repentance; to dedicate myself again to thee, my Savior; to exercise my faith in thy atoning blood and justifying righteousness; and to pour forth my supplications for pardoning mercy and sanctifying grace. May it be a sweet and refreshing season to my soul, and to the souls of all communicants! May we meet with the Lord our Redeemer at his table, and enjoy communion with him, and with one another! Grant my prayer, for thy name's sake. Amen.

Meditation 2

The Cross of Christ

How wonderful the object presented by the ordinance of the Lord's supper for the contemplation of the invited guests! Nothing less than the Son of God nailed to the accursed cross, dying in shame and ignominy, bearing our sins and the wrath of the Almighty, to satisfy the demands of his justice, and thus make full expiation for them. "Behold the Lamb of God that taketh away the sin of the world!" (John 1:29).

In vain shall we search elsewhere for such a spectacle. Its like is not to be found in any other part of the universe. This earth, cursed as it is by sin, has alone, of all the worlds in the boundless dominions of the Almighty, been blessed and honored with the amazing spectacle.

Taught by the first great promise announced to our first parents, immediately after their fall, concerning the Seed of the woman, who was to bruise the serpent's head, our apostate race began, from the beginning, to expect a deliverer from the ruin that sin had brought on the world. With the revolution of ages, as new light was imparted, by prophecy and promise, to the Church, believers were sustained in their expectations, and were enabled to look, through the types and ceremonies, with greater clearness, for the coming of the Messiah. Thus were the eyes of the whole Church, and their longing expectations, directed to Him, till his advent in the flesh.

And since his appearance in the world, and the accomplishment of his mighty work on earth, the eyes of the Church have been turned to his cross, and will be turned to it, to the end of time, as the great object of their faith, and the source of their redemption. To it they look, and will look, for peace, and comfort, and hope, and joy, and eternal life.

From the first intimation of God's merciful designs towards our fallen world, angels, those holy and exalted creatures that inhabit heaven, and stand around the throne of the Most High, have felt a deep interest in the mystery of redemption. With delight they have, in all ages, ministered unto the heirs of salvation. How joyfully they announced the Savior's birth to the shepherds on the fields of Bethlehem, and sang the song, "Glory to God in the highest; and on earth, peace, good-will toward men" (Luke 2:14). When Jesus had in the wilderness repelled the tempter, the Evangelist says, "Behold, angels came and ministered unto him;" and another Evangelist says, after narrating his agony in the garden, "And there appeared an angel from heaven, strengthening him" (Matthew 4:11; Luke 22:43). At his resurrection, the angel of the Lord descended from heaven, and rolling back from the sepulcher the stone, sat upon it, with a countenance like lightning, and raiment white as snow, terrifying the Roman guard, so that they became as dead men. And when our Lord ascended to heaven, two angels assured his wondering disciples, that he would hereafter come again, in like manner as they saw him go into heaven. And ever since, these exalted spirits have employed their mighty intellects in studying the great mystery of redemption; for Peter, when speaking of the salvation of Christ, says, "which things the angels desire to look into" (1 Peter 1:12).

Still more is the cross of Christ to be magnified: for the eye of God himself has, from the ages of eternity, rested upon it, as the development of that great mystery of his will, that is to fill this world, heaven itself, and all other worlds, with the fullest exhibition of his glory. The cross is the center of Jehovah's moral government. Here peace is made between heaven and earth. "For he is our peace, who hath made both one, and hath broken down the middle wall of partition between us; having abolished in his flesh the enmity, even the law of commandments contained in ordinances; for to make in himself of twain one new man, so making peace; and that he might reconcile both unto God in one body by the cross, having slain the enmity thereby: and came and preached to you which were afar off, and to them that were nigh. For through him we both have access by one Spirit unto the Father." And "in the dispensation of the fulness of time God will gather in one all things in Christ, both which are in heaven, and which are on earth, even in him; of whom the whole family in heaven and earth is named" (Ephesians 2:14-18; 1:10; 3:15).

From the cross of Christ an influence has gone forth, that has been felt by the affairs of mankind, both before and since his coming into the world. In reference to it a whole nation was selected by God, as his chosen people, and a place prepared for them among the nations of the earth. They were guarded by a peculiar and miraculous providence, and instructed by a long line of inspired teachers and prophets. The affairs of other nations were controlled by a regard to the cross; and so extensive dominion was given to the Roman empire, that the way might be prepared for the preaching of the cross, and the establishment of the Church in the Gentile world.

Ever since, the affairs of nations have felt the influence of this wonderful transaction. They have prospered, or declined, as they regarded, or disregarded the gospel of Christ crucified. And hereafter the cross will be lifted up on high; and to it will all nations flock as the fountain of peace, of life, of holiness, of happiness, and of glory.

And the cross will be the object of delightful contemplation and profound study, and the subject of joyous conversation, to redeemed saints and to holy angels, throughout the endless ages of eternity; and forever will be sung in heaven by the ransomed ones the song, "Unto him that loved us and washed us in his own blood, and hath made us kings and priests unto God and his Father; to him be glory and dominion for ever and ever. Amen" (Revelation 1:5-6).

The cross of Jesus Christ is the center, which throws its light on the whole circle of divine truth. Here, then, at the foot of the cross of my

Lord and Savior, let me stand, and look around. What a circle of rich and invaluable truths meets my eyes! I see all the great and leading facts and truths of divine revelation. The apostasy of our race—the superiority of the Christian dispensation—the glory of God shining in the face of Christ—the divine person of our Redeemer—his infinite condescension and profound humiliation—his holy life, and painful sufferings and agonizing death—his triumphant resurrection and glorious ascension into heaven—his session at God's right hand and intercession there—his coming again to judge the world, and consummate the salvation of his people—the all-sufficiency of his atonement and righteousness, and rich and invaluable benefits—his free and boundless love—the evil of sin—the duty of self-examination and self-dedication—all these facts and truths are connected with, and illustrated by, the cross of Christ. These are the topics on which it is proper for Christians to meditate in preparing their minds and hearts for an acceptable and profitable approach to the Lord's table.

What attractions in the cross of my Redeemer! Gaze, my soul, at it, with wonder and delight. Look at it again and again. Never lose sight of it. Behold the glory of it, that thou mayest be assimilated into its likeness.

PRAYER

Most High and holy God, may I love to contemplate the cross of thy Son! How amazing the spectacle! In infinite mercy thou wast pleased to honor our fallen world, by making it the seal of a transaction more wonderful, than any to be found in any other world in thy vast dominions. Before the eyes of our rebellious race, thou hast lifted up thy well-beloved Son, agonizing and dying on the cross, as the appointed sacrifice for sin, that they might look to it, and be healed of their wounds, and live.

Oh! Grant that my eyes may ever be directed to this wonderful spectacle. May I never forget it, but gaze at it with increasing delight. May I understand the great design for which my Lord and Savior was covered with ignominy, and died in pain and agony; and thus, by faith, see a glory beaming forth from the cross of insufferable brightness. May I there behold the most illustrious exhibition of thy glory, and the great salvation provided for our rebellions race. May I see how the cross is connected with, and throws its light upon, the great truths and facts recorded in the Bible. May I contemplate it as the grand center of all thy dispensations towards the children of men; as the source of peace and friendship, of holiness and happiness; as uniting all holy beings in heaven and on earth into one glorious society under Christ as the blessed Head. Beholding the glory of the cross, may I be changed into the same image, from glory to glory, even by the Spirit of our God. May I embrace the cross by faith, and glory in nothing but the cross; and feel it crucifying the world to me, and lifting my affections above all its allurements, honors and pleasures; and setting them on heavenly objects, where my Savior reigns in ineffable glory. Hear me, O Lord, for Christ's sake. Amen.

Meditation 3

The Apostasy of the Human Race

When we look at the cross, and behold the Son of God expiring on it, we are naturally led to inquire after the cause of that wonderful event. Why did He suffer and die? He was perfectly free from sin, and was holy, both in heart and in life. He loved his Father, and always did his will; and he was beloved of his Father, who delighted in him as his only begotten Son. He could not then suffer for his own sins; for he had none. Yet he suffered and suffered dreadfully. Why? There was a sufficient cause; so that the Father, while he loved him most endearingly, could, consistently with this love which he never ceased to feel towards him, and consistently with his justice, afflict and bruise him, and put him to grief and shame. What was that cause? The apostle Peter answers the question, as the prophet Isaiah had done ages before. When, speaking of the Redeemer, he says: "Who his own self bare our sins in his own body on the tree, that we, being dead to sins, should live unto God; for Christ also hath suffered for sins, the just for the unjust, that he might bring us to God" (1 Peter 2:24; 3:18).

Here is the reason of the amazing spectacle, exhibited on mount Calvary to the view of the world. The sins of mankind were the cause. Had not man apostatized from God and brought ruin on himself and all his posterity, that amazing spectacle would never have been seen by our eyes. It was to redeem us from just, deserved, and helpless ruin and misery, that the Savior bled and died upon the cross.

That man is a fallen, sinful, guilty creature, we find the most abundant and convincing proof. Of this mournful fact I am surrounded daily with incontestable evidences. I look at my friends and acquaintances, and what do I see? Unfallen, sinless creatures? Not one such can I find. All exhibit marks of depravity. What forgetfulness of God and disregard of his favor, and violations of his holy commandments, do I see? Some indeed are penitent and believing, the disciples of Christ, and friends of God. But they are imperfectly sanctified, and most ready to acknowledge the native depravity of their hearts, and to lament their remaining imperfections and failures in duty. The rest, with few exceptions, are moving on in the journey of life, unprepared for death, and thoughtless of a judgment to come.

Wherever I go, and however I extend my intercourse with my fellow creatures, I find the same evidence of human depravity. What mean our courts of justice, our prisons and penitentiaries, the bolts and bars by which we secure our houses? What mean diseases, famine, pestilence, and death? Are they not all proofs of human depravity?

What is the history of mankind, but a history of wars, bloodshed and crimes? Where, in any part of its universal pages, can be found the history of any portion of our race, however small, who have lived in the love of God, and in love to one another, free from selfishness and covetousness, envy and ambition, lust and impurity—passions that everywhere are seen working out crimes and misery in this fallen world?

If I open the Bible, I see, from the beginning to the end of its inspired pages, the plainest proofs of the fall and sinfulness of man. In the first pages, written by Moses, I see, that Adam was created upright, in the image and likeness of his Creator. He was a holy, sinless, and happy creature, rejoicing in the favor and love of God. But soon, through the power of temptation, which he had ample power to resist, he fell from his holy and happy condition, by transgressing the commandment of his God. I read the sentence pronounced on him and his guilty companion, by their offended Maker and righteous Judge. I see them expelled in anger from their delightful garden, and compelled to labor and toil, and eat their bread in the sweat of their brow. Oh! If they had not sinned, this whole earth would have been one extended garden of delights, in which their holy posterity would have been seen living under the smiles of their God! But, alas! Children are born to the guilty pair; and soon it becomes manifest, that they are like their common parents, depraved. "The Lord had respect unto Abel and to his offering; but unto Cain and to his offering he had not respect" (Genesis 4:4-5). Moved by envy at the preference which God was pleased to show to his younger brother, Cain wickedly slew him.

The human race is multiplied; and, with the increase of men, wickedness is so multiplied, that Moses writes, "And it repented the Lord that he had made man on the earth, and it grieved him at his heart" (Genesis 6:6). God determines to bring a flood upon an ungodly world. It comes, and sweeps away, with the besom of destruction, the whole race of sinners, with the exception of Noah and his family. What an awful monument of human depravity and of God's righteous indignation against sin!

The history of Noah's descendants, written with the pen of inspiration, discovers the same stream of depravity flowing through every generation. That peculiar people, separated by God's providence from the rest of mankind, for the maintenance of his worship and religion in the world, forms no exception. Throughout their whole history, written by inspired men, I see the most incontestable evidence of the great wickedness of the human heart.

I read the epistle of the apostle Paul to the Romans, and what increasing evidence is presented of the apostasy and ruin of our race! How deplorable the description he gives of the great wickedness of Gentile nations, (chapter 1) and how clearly he proves, from their own scriptures, (chapter 2, 3) that the Jews were no better! How conclusive his argument, that no flesh can be justified by the works of the law before God; and that all, without exception, stand in perishing need of the redemption of Jesus Christ; whose righteousness by faith "is unto all and upon all them that believe; for there is no difference: for all have sinned, and come short of the glory of God" (Romans 3:20-31).

My soul, what overwhelming evidence is here of the apostasy, depravity, and ruin of the race of creatures to which I belong! And does not my personal history prove most clearly that I am involved in guilt, sin, and misery? How soon evidence of my depraved heart appeared! What selfishness, envy, evil desires, began early to work within my bosom, and bring forth the deeds of sin! How forgetful of God, and his service! How wandering have been my thoughts and eyes in his sanctuary! How can I answer for the guilt contracted, in times past, in this manner, while professedly hearing his blessed word, and presenting worship to infinite Majesty? How long I lived without God, and without Christ in the world! How, while thus estranged from my Creator, and following the wayward inclinations of my heart, did my corruption increase in strength! And had not the restraints of his providence and grace held me back, to what lengths of iniquity might I not have gone! And into what depths of guilt might I not have plunged! Ah! How much I needed the redemption of Jesus Christ! What eye but his pitied me in my fallen condition; and what arm but his could deliver me from the terrible pit into which I had fallen? What blood but his could wash away my guilt, and what but his spotless righteousness could cover my nakedness, and render so polluted and vile a sinner acceptable in the sight of infinite purity! And although I am permitted to entertain the hope of having been renewed and sanctified by divine grace, yet I feel the workings of much evil in my heart, and a proneness to wander from my God. Blessed Jesus, I commit myself to thee. Cleanse me daily from my sins by thy blood. Keep around me the glorious robe of thy righteousness. Guide me by thy Spirit. Strengthen me by thy grace. Defend me by thy power. Perfect thy work in me; and bring me safely to thy heavenly kingdom. Amen.

Prayer

Most Holy God, when I look to the cross of my Redeemer, I see the most convincing evidence of the fall of our race; for had not man been guilty and depraved, that wonderful spectacle on Calvary would never have been witnessed on the earth.

All my friends and acquaintances I find to be corrupt in their nature. All are sinners. Nowhere can I find an individual who is free from sin. The whole frame of civil society attests the mournful fact, that our race is apostate from God, by the provision it makes for restraining the hand of violence, and punishing crimes. And thou, most righteous Jehovah, hast, in thy providence, by the various diseases and calamities brought upon the world, proclaimed the mournful truth, that thou art angry with us for our rebellious conduct; and in thy word thou hast taught us the origin of our depravity, and exposed to view the polluted fountain that has sent forth its bitter and poisonous streams over all the earth, and through every nation under heaven.

And when I look into my own heart, I see how vile it is; what lusts and wicked passions have defiled it, and prompted those sinful acts that have disgraced my life. How much it becomes me to lie in the dust at thy feet, O my offended Creator, and to implore thy forgiving mercy! Deeply impress my mind, I beseech thee, with an abiding conviction of my native depravity and contracted guilt; that I may always feel my need of the atoning blood and cleansing grace of Jesus Christ. Forgive my sins, and sanctify my nature, for his sake. Amen.

Meditation 4

The Superiority of the Christian Dispensation

Before the wonderful scene on Calvary had been exhibited to the view of the Church, and while Jesus yet lived on the earth, he said to his apostles, "Blessed are your eyes, for they see: and your ears, for they hear. For verily I say unto you, that many prophets and righteous men have desired to see those things which ye see, and have not seen them; and to hear those things which ye hear, and have not heard them" (Matthew 13:16-17). And yet, at that time, the apostles were so imperfectly enlightened in regard to the great facts of the gospel, that, when Jesus spake of his approaching death and resurrection, they could not understand his meaning. (See Matthew 15:21-23, Mark 9:31, 32, Luke 18:31-34.) Subsequently to the Savior's death, when the apostles had been fully enlightened in the mysteries of the gospel, Peter writes "Of which salvation the prophets have inquired and searched diligently, who prophesied of the grace that should come unto you: searching what, or what manner of time, the Spirit of Christ which was in them did signify, when it testified beforehand the sufferings of Christ, and the glory that should follow. Unto whom it was revealed, that not unto themselves, but unto us they did minister the things, which are now reported unto you by them which have preached the gospel unto you with the Holy Ghost sent down from heaven; which things the angels desire to look into" (1 Peter 1:10-12).

The Jews looked through types, sacrifices and ceremonies, predictions and promises, and saw dimly and obscurely, the great events that have been set before us in the clearest light. And even the prophets who were inspired to foretell these great events, studied their own prophecies, that they might understand the import of the words they uttered, under the dictation of the Holy Spirit; but they were unable to discover it; and were instructed by the Spirit, that the favor sought by them was reserved for the Church, when their predictions should be fulfilled. The Jews had the types; we have the realization of the types: they had the sacrifices; we, the end, the great sacrifice, to which they pointed: they studied the prophecies; we their fulfillment. The Jews had the sign; we the thing signified: they enjoyed the shadow; we the substance. On them the day dawned dimly; on us it sheds its meridian light.

The Jews looked for a Savior, who was to come, whose character, offices and work they imperfectly understood. We look to a Savior, who has come, assumed his several offices and accomplished his glorious work. We have seen him come into the world, appear in our nature, live, and suffer, and die; and then rise from the dead, ascend into heaven, take his seat at the right hand of God, and reign Head over all things for his Church. The plan of salvation has been completely unfolded to our view; the way to heaven plainly marked out before our eyes. We are told, in the plainest words, what we are to believe and do to be saved; that for salvation we are to rely, not on our own works, but on the atonement and righteousness of Christ.

So superior is the Christian dispensation in light; and equally distinguished is it by the measure of the Spirit granted to us who live under it. "This spake he of the Spirit which they that believe on him should receive: for the Holy Ghost was not yet given, because that Jesus was not yet glorified" (John 7:39). This passage is not to be understood as if it meant that the Spirit had not been heretofore imparted to the children of men. In every age he has wrought by his common and special grace. He was the life of the Church in all periods, and under every dispensation. This awful warning is early found on the records of inspiration: "My Spirit shall not always strive with man" (Genesis 6:3). It only means that a much larger measure of the Spirit was to be imparted under the approaching economy, that was to bless the Church, after the exaltation of her glorious Head. This was the coronation gift of her ascended King, most munificently bestowed on the apostles and other disciples, that qualified them for the work of founding and edifying the Christian Church; a gift still bestowed on the Church since that blessed day, in every successive age, in a greater or less degree.

The present dispensation is characterized too by *superior privileges* bestowed on the Church. The ancient Church was indeed, compared with other nations, near unto God, who had taken her into covenant relation, and denominated Israel his chosen; yet she was kept at a distance, and subject to carnal ordinances, and a yoke hard to bear. But once a year the high priest alone of all the chosen tribes, was permitted to enter into the most holy place, with blood, which he offered for himself and for the errors of the people; a restriction by which the Holy Ghost signified "that the way into the holiest of all was not yet made manifest" (Hebrews 9:7-8). But since the one offering of our great High Priest, "by which he hath perfected forever them that are sanctified" (Hebrews 10:14), the way into the holiest is made manifest, and every believing Christian has liberty to enter into that most sacred place, not once in a year, but daily; and by prayer and supplication converse with infinite Majesty, seated on the mercy seat. What a privilege! Come, then, my soul, relying on thy great High Priest, "boldly unto the throne of grace, to obtain mercy, and find grace to help in time of need" (Hebrews 10:19-22; 4:14-16).

Corresponding with this precious privilege of prayer, is the *filial temper* that distinguishes the present dispensation. The worship of ancient saints, owing to the imperfection of the economy under which they lived, was marred by servile fear. Not such is Christian worship. That, by the aid of the Holy Spirit, is offered with a filial temper. "For," says Paul, "ye have not received the spirit of bondage again to fear; but ye have received the Spirit of adoption, whereby we cry, Abba, Father. The Spirit itself beareth witness with our spirits, that we are the children of God" (Romans 8:15-

16). Jesus Christ redeems his people from the law, that they may receive the adoption of sons; "And because ye are sons," says Paul, "God hath sent forth the Spirit of his Son into your hearts, crying, Abba, Father. Wherefore thou art no more a servant, but a son; and if a son, then an heir of God through Christ" (Galatians 4:4-7).

Finally, the Christian dispensation is distinguished, by brighter hopes in reference to the future world. Ancient believers were acquainted with the great facts, the resurrection of the body, and a life to come. But an inspired writer, speaking of Jesus Christ, writes, "Who hath abolished death, and hath brought life and immortality to light through the gospel" (2 Timothy 1:10). How plain the instructions of the great Teacher! "Marvel not at this: for the hour is coming, in the which all that are in the graves shall hear his voice, and shall come forth: they that have done good, unto the resurrection of life; and they that have done evil, unto the resurrection of damnation" (John 5:28-29). "My sheep hear my voice and they follow me; and I give unto them eternal life; and they shall never perish, neither shall any pluck them out of my hands" (John 10:27-28). "Let not your hearts be troubled: ye believe in God, believe also in me. In my Father's house are many mansions: if it were not so, I would have told you. I go to prepare a place for you. And if I go and prepare a place for you, I will come again, and receive you to myself; that where I am, there ye may be also" (John 14:1-3). How many passages of Scripture might be here repeated! (See 2 Timothy 4:6-8, 1 Corinthians 15:42-58, 2 Corinthians 5:1-8.)

So superior in light—in the *gift* of the Spirit—in privileges, in *free* and *filial* intercourse with God—and in hope of future blessedness, is the Christian dispensation! Comparing the ministration of the law with the ministration of the Spirit, the apostle says, in conclusion, "For if the ministration of condemnation be glory, much more doth the ministration of righteousness exceed in glory. For even that which was made glorious had no glory in this respect, by reason of the glory that excelleth. For if that which was done away was glorious, much more that which remaineth is glorious" (2 Corinthians 3:6-11).

Thus highly favored, living under such a dispensation of light and privileges, of the Spirit, and of immortal hopes, how should Christians be distinguished by a conduct pure and heavenly! Awake, my soul, shake off thy slumbers and sluggishness, and strive to act up to thy privileges. Show thy gratitude to God for what he has done for thee. Live by faith. Aspire after a better world. Be humble and holy, watchful and heavenly. Endeavor to shine as a light in this dark world. Prepare to meet thy coming Savior and Lord.

PRAYER

Merciful God, I bless thee that thou wast pleased to give me birth under the new and better dispensation of grace. Thou hast greatly distinguished the Christian, above thine ancient Church. I praise thee for that superior light and those richer spiritual influences, which thou hast bestowed on thy people under the present economy. I bless thee for those superior privileges, and the adoption of sons which thou hast vouchsafed to us; that we are no longer kept at a distance from thee, but are permitted to come into the holiest of all, through the rent veil, that is, the flesh of Christ, and make the nearest approach to thy Majesty on the mercy-seat, and converse with thee by prayer, thanksgiving, and praise, with confidence of a gracious audience, and the assurance of a merciful answer. I thank thee for the spirit of adoption, to form our hearts to a filial temper, and to enable us to call thee "Abba, Father." I bless thee for those brighter hopes which thou dost inspire in our hearts, by the clearer revelation which than hast afforded in regard to a future world, and by the better promises of the gospel of our Redeemer.

Grant me grace, I beseech thee, my heavenly Father, duly to appreciate the state in which thou hast been pleased to place me, and carefully to improve these superior and distinguishing privileges. Let me live near to my God, and enjoy that sweet and delightful intercourse, which I am invited to cherish and cultivate. Give me, I entreat thee, a spiritual and heavenly mind. Call off my affections from things below, and set them on things above. Let the same mind be in me that was in Christ Jesus. Hear me, for his sake. Amen.

MEDITATION 5

THE GLORY OF GOD IN THE CROSS

In the cross of Christ, how does the glory of God shine! "God, who commanded the light to shine out of darkness, hath shined into our hearts to give the light of the knowledge of the glory of God in the face of Jesus Christ" (2 Corinthians 4:4).

The glory of God is his perfections; where these are seen, his glory is seen. He loves his own glory; and the great end of all his works, is the exhibition of his glory, or the display of his infinite perfections. His perfections accordingly are exhibited in creation and providence; but more clearly and fully (and especially his moral attributes) in redemption.

His wisdom, for example, is exhibited in creation. In the arrangement of land and water; in the structure of the earth, as a habitation for man, and the various orders of inferior creatures; in the senses and organs of human bodies, and the adaptation of light and other objects to the eye, and of sounds to the ear; in the formation of the tongue and lips for articulate enunciation of the voice; in the constitution and position of the sun in our system, for imparting light and heat to this earth and her sister planets; and in ten thousand other particulars that might be mentioned, the wisdom of God is manifested. So, in the provision made by divine Providence for the sustentation and nourishment of men and other creatures, and in controlling and superintending their actions, the same attribute is displayed.

But in the work of redemption God has made a brighter exhibition of his wisdom. In the person of the Redeemer, in his mediation, in his substitution in the sinner's place, and in the result of his sufferings and death, there is a wonderful display of infinite wisdom. The plan of salvation was far beyond the conception of created intelligence. None could tell whether the salvation of fallen man was possible. To heavenly beings he appeared forever ruined by his apostasy. But, behold, the infinite mind brings forth the wonderous scheme, by which every obstacle in the way of his restoration to the divine favor, and the recovery of his lost holiness, is removed. Justice is satisfied, and the sinner saved. Sin is pardoned, and yet sin is punished. The rebel is released, and yet government is maintained. God is glorified, while he exercises his boundless mercy in forgiving and saving guilty and rebellious creatures, who had ungratefully broken his laws, and daringly insulted his infinite majesty.

The justice of God has been signally displayed in his dealings with our race. In the expulsion of our first parents from paradise; in the curse pronounced that caused the earth to bring forth thorns and thistles, and to demand from man laborious culture, in order to obtain its fruits; in the general and overwhelming deluge; in the fires of Sodom and Gomorrah; in wars, famine, and pestilence; in diseases and death, justice is fearfully displayed. And it may be seen in all its fearful terrors in the fires kindled up for tormenting devils and lost men.

But in the cross, in the sufferings and death of Jesus Christ, God has given the strongest and the most convincing demonstration of his strict and inflexible justice. There we see, that sin cannot escape punishment; that the claims of justice must be satisfied, or the sinner cannot be pardoned. God "spared not his own Son, but delivered him up for us all" (Romans 8:32). The cup of suffering could not pass from his lips. He drank up its very dregs. Nothing was abated in his favor. A full equivalent of sufferings was exacted from him. How awful is divine justice when we look at the cross! Let sinners tremble. And thou, my soul, stand in awe of this frowning attribute of thy God!

How delightfully shines forth in the cross of our Redeemer the love of God! That God is a benevolent being we have ample proof in creation and in providence. The production of innumerable sensitive creatures, endowed with various capacities for enjoyment; the provision made for satisfying their diversified appetites and desires; the senses of the human body, which are so many sources of pleasure; the endearing relations constituted, by divine wisdom, in domestic life, between husbands and wives, parents and children, brothers and sisters; the structure and intercourse of social life; and the numerous sources of enjoyment opened in creation and providence—all proclaim the benevolence of the Almighty.

But in redemption we see his amazing goodness and mercy. He is seen to be not only benevolent, but to be Love. "God so loved the world, that he gave his only begotten Son, that whosoever believeth in him, should not perish, but have everlasting life." "In this was manifested the love of God toward us, because that God sent his only begotten Son into the world, that we might live through him. Herein is love, not that we loved God, but that he loved us, and sent his Son to be the propitiation for our sins." "Behold, what manner of love the Father hath bestowed upon us, that we should be called the sons of God." "But God commendeth his love toward us, in that, while we were yet sinners, Christ died for us" (John 3:16; 1 John 4:10; 3:1; Romans 5:8). In such warm language the sacred writers speak on this animating subject.

Benevolence to unoffending creatures is not surprising. The goodness of the Creator towards first parents, while in a state of innocence, and his signal favors bestowed on holy angels, call for the warmest gratitude and praise. But his pardoning mercy and distinguishing love shown to our fallen face, how wonderful! When we consider the condition of sinful man, that he had apostatized from his Creator, and rendered himself guilty and vile by his pollution; that he was in a state of enmity to God, and felt no disposition to return, but was wandering more and more from his God; that, while in this state, an object, not of mercy, but of incensed justice, his offended sovereign should not only pity, but set his love upon him when there was no way for his redemption, but by the humiliation, and sufferings, and death of his own beloved Son; how amazing is it, that the ever blessed Jehovah, who stood in no need of the service of our miserable race, but could, with a word, have called another world into existence, filled with nobler creatures, and established in holiness, to rejoice in his favors, and to delight in offering the homage of grateful and loving hearts, and continual and lofty praise, to him from whom they received their being, and all their endowments and blessedness; how amazing that the all sufficient Jehovah, whose name would have been unblemished, if he had left us to perish in our sins, should freely love us, and determine, in a way so extraordinary, to save us, and raise us to happiness and glory, greater than we should have attained if we had never sinned!

In this illustrious manner, the glory of God, his wisdom, justice, and love, shine forth in the cross of Jesus Christ, his own Son. Dwell, my soul, upon this glorious subject. Meditate upon it again and again, that thou mayest feel its transforming influence, by inflaming thy love, awakening thy penitence, increasing thy zeal, and exciting thy desires for holiness in heart and life. "But we all, with open face, beholding as in a glass, the glory of the Lord, are changed into the same image from glory to glory, even as by the Spirit of the Lord" (2 Corinthians 3:18). The glory of God assimilates into his own likeness those who contemplate it. Let me love the glory of God, and contemplate it, with the eye of faith, that I may participate in its assimilating influences, and by the light and grace of the Holy Spirit, be changed into the glorious image of my God.

PRAYER

Great and Almighty God, I praise thee for the display of thy glory in thy works, and especially for that brighter exhibition of it in the cross of Jesus Christ. I see thy wisdom in the arrangements of creation, and in the order of thy providence; but I see thy wisdom more illustriously displayed in the salvation of fallen man, by the sufferings and death of thine own Son.

Thy justice has been terribly manifested by the judgments inflicted on our apostate race; but how much more fearfully manifested was it in the punishment inflicted on thy well beloved Son, for the sins of his people! Thou hast shown thy benevolence in the production of so many sensitive creatures of various capacities for enjoyment, and in the provision made for supplying them with appropriate pleasures; but in the plan of redemption, and in the gift of thy Son for our salvation, thou hast unfolded thy heart, and shown thyself to be LOVE.

Oh! May I love to trace thy perfections in thy works and ways, but especially as they shine in the work of redemption. May I love the glory of my God; and, by contemplating it, may I find myself changed into thy blessed image, inspired with hatred of sin, and with love to holiness. May I long for that bright display of thy glory which beams around the spirits of just men made perfect, and fills them with unutterable blessedness, and calls forth rapturous songs of praise to God and the Lamb. Grant my prayer, for Jesus' sake. Amen.

MEDITATION 6

THE PERSON OF OUR REDEEMER

How important is it for me and others, to know the true character of our Redeemer! We ought to understand well the foundation on which we rest our hopes for eternity; and to be assured, that he to whom we commit our immortal interests, is fully able to secure them against all dangers.

Who, my soul, is he to whom thou hast committed thyself? Is he able to sustain the high office of Mediator between offended Majesty and his offending and rebellious creatures? Can he atone for thy sins, and the sins of the world? Can he furnish thee and all who confide in him, with that perfect righteousness which the law demands, and without which no sinner can be admitted into heaven? Is he able to deliver thee out of the hands of all those malignant enemies, who seek thy ruin, and bring thee safely to his eternal kingdom? Is there sufficient reason to warrant thee to place the most unlimited confidence in him for everything that thou canst need or desire? Blessed be God, there are ample grounds for such confidence! Rejoice, my soul; thou mayest safely trust in thy Redeemer. He has all power to save thee, and all who trust in him.

But let me review the grounds of my hope, and thus strengthen my faith. Who is my Redeemer? He is just what the exigencies of my condition require. He is GOD and MAN in one DIVINE PERSON.

I look to the cross, and there I behold one in human form; nailed to the accursed tree; bleeding and dying in shame and ignominy. Can I doubt that he was a man, when he was seen as such by every eye that saw him suspended on the cross? His body was scourged by Pilate's orders; his temples torn by a crown of thorns; his hands and feet were nailed to the cross; his body was then lifted up on the cross to be thrust violently into the place prepared, that he might die a lingering and agonizing death; and his side was afterwards pierced with a spear. From the wound came forth blood and water; sure proofs of his death. "Behold my hands and feet," said he to his terrified disciples, who imagined him to be a spirit, "that it is I myself: handle me, and see; for a spirit hath not flesh and bones, as ye see me have" (Luke 24:39).

I read the gospels, and there I learn, that my Redeemer was conceived by the Holy Ghost in the womb of a virgin, born in the appointed time, and bound, like other human infants, in swaddling bands. Like other men he ate and drank, hungered and thirsted, became weary and needed rest. He slept and awoke, walked and conversed with his disciples. In a word he had all the properties and sinless infirmities of human nature. I learn that he had too a rational soul, endowed with faculties of understanding, will, and affections. Of him it is written: "And Jesus increased in wisdom and stature, and in favor with God and man" (Luke 2:52). Of himself he said in the garden of Gethsemane, "My SOUL is exceeding sorrowful, even unto death."

But, while my Redeemer possessed a perfect human nature, a reasonable soul, as well as an organized body like other men, and denominated himself by the title, "SON OF MAN," he was perfectly holy, and free from all sin.

Jesus was indeed a man; for, if he had not possessed our nature, he could not have been subject to the law that was given to our race, nor been our substitute.

But he was infinitely more than a mere man. He was "God over all blessed forever" (Romans 9:5). Of this great truth, the Godhead of my Redeemer, I find in scripture the most abundant proof. In this character he was revealed to God's ancient church. He was the angel who went before the chosen tribes, and led them through the wilderness; of whom Jehovah said, "Beware of him, and obey his voice, provoke him not; for he will not pardon your transgressions; for MY NAME is in him" (Exodus

23:20-21). Speaking of him, David, uttering the address of Jehovah to him, says, "I will declare the decree: the Lord hath said unto me, THOU ART MY SON. *This day have I begotten thee*" (Psalm 2:7). Thus, before Jesus was born, he was styled the Son of God. The Jews understood the import of this lofty title; for when our Savior assumed it, by calling God his Father, in a peculiar sense, they sought to kill him; because, by asserting his filial relation to God, he made himself equal to God (John 5:17-23). What lofty titles does Isaiah apply to the Redeemer! "For unto us a child is born, unto us a son is given: and the government shall be upon his shoulder: and his name shall be called Wonderful, Counselor, The mighty God, The everlasting Father, The Prince of Peace" (Isaiah 9:6).

In many passages that incommunicable name JEHOVAH, which cannot be applied to any creature however exalted, is by this prophet and others given to the Redeemer. (See Isaiah 14:20-25, 48:17, 51:9-11, 54:5; Hosea 1:7; Zechariah 2:10-11.)

Such is a specimen of the testimonies of the Old Testament to the Divinity of the Messiah. But when I read the pages of the New Testament, how full, and plain, and explicit, the testimonies of the inspired writers to this great truth! John begins his gospel thus: "In the beginning was the Word, and the Word was with God, and the Word was God. The same was in the beginning with God. All things were made by him; and without him was not any thing made that was made. In him was life; and the life was the light of men" (John 1:1-4). "And the Word was made flesh, and dwelt among us (and we beheld his glory, the glory as of the only begotten of the Father), full of grace and truth" (verse 14). Paul, in his epistle to the Colossians, speaks of the Redeemer in this lofty manner: "Who is the image of the invisible God, the first born of every creature. For by him were all things created that are in heaven, and that are in earth, visible and invisible, whether they be thrones or dominions, or principalities, or powers: all things were created by him, and for him: and he is before all things, and by him all things consist" (Colossians 1:15-17). Again, in his epistle to the Philippians: "Who, being in the form of God, thought it not robbery to be equal with God." "That at the name of Jesus every knee should bow, of things in heaven and things in earth, and things under the earth; and that every tongue should confess that Jesus Christ is Lord, to the glory of God the Father" (Philippians 2:6, 10-11). In similar terms he speaks, in his epistle to the Hebrews: "God, who at sundry times and in divers manners, spake in time past, unto the fathers by the prophets, hath in these last days spoken unto us by his Son, whom he hath appointed heir of all things, by whom also he made the worlds; who being the brightness of his glory and the express image of his person, and upholding all things by the word of his power, when he had by himself purged our sins, sat down on the right hand of the Majesty on high" (Hebrews 1:1-3). And in the book of Revelation the whole creation are represented as worshiping Jesus Christ, the Lamb (Revelation 5:11-14).

How full, how strong, how abundant the testimonies, both of the Old and of the New Testament, to the Godhead of our Redeemer! Not a doubt should remain on the mind, that he is "God over all, blessed forever."

But it is not to be forgotten, that he is God and man in ONE PERSON. His human nature had no personality of its own; because it never existed by itself, apart from the divine nature. From the first moment of its existence it was taken into union with the divine nature; and of course was absorbed by a divine person, and became a complex portion of a divine person. The prophet Isaiah says, "Behold, a virgin shall conceive, and bear a son, and his name shall be called Immanuel;" that is, God with us (Isaiah 7:14). The apostle Paul exclaims, "And without controversy, great is the mystery of godliness: God was manifest in the flesh" (1 Timothy 3:16). This hypostatic union of the two natures, justifies the language used by our Lord to Nicodemus: "And no man hath ascended up to heaven, but he that came down from heaven, even *the Son of man* WHICH IS IN HEAVEN" (John 3:13), and that of Paul: "The church of God which he purchased WITH HIS OWN BLOOD" (Acts 20:28).

How perfectly was the character of our Savior adapted to the office of Mediator, which he assumed, and the work of redemption which he undertook! As man he could be subject to law, obey and suffer; and as God he could sustain his human nature under any amount of sufferings; while the infinite dignity of his person imparted an infinite value to his sufferings and obedience, and rendered them a full equivalent for the sufferings due to all who shall be saved, and furnished a perfect righteousness sufficient to justify all who believe, and entitle them to everlasting life.

With what unlimited confidence may I commit my eternal interests into his hands! And what abundant reason have I to adopt the apostle's language: "I know in whom I have believed, and am persuaded that he is able to keep that which I have committed unto him against that day" (2 Timothy 1:12). In coming to him, I am chargeable with neither impiety nor folly; for I come home, by committing myself to my God, and in devoting myself to him, I only perform what duty and gratitude prompt and constrain me to do: "for to this end Christ both died, and revived, and rose again, that he might be Lord both of the dead and of the living" (Romans 14:9). "For the Father judgeth no man, but hath committed all judgment unto the Son; that all men might honor the Son, even as they honor the Father. He that honoreth not the Son, honoreth not the Father which hath sent him" (John 5:22-23).

PRAYER

Great and merciful God, I adore thee for providing for our fallen race a glorious Mediator, who could interpose between us and our offended

Sovereign, and avert from us his terrible wrath. I extol thy infinite wisdom, displayed in the wonderful constitution of his PERSON. I bless thee for the abundant proof of the reality of his human nature; that he possessed both an organized body and a reasonable soul; so that he could be made subject to the law of our race, and both obey its precepts, and endure its penalty. I rejoice to know, that, being perfectly holy, and free from sin, he did obey the law, in the most faultless manner; and that he did endure its penalty in its utmost extent; so as to make an ample atonement for sin, and to work out a complete righteousness, for the full justification of every true believer.

I bless thee, O God, for the ample testimony of thy word to assure us, that our Redeemer was infinitely more than man; being the second person in the adorable Trinity, God over all, blessed forever; Immanuel, God with us, God manifest in the flesh, God and man in one divine person; and thus able to sustain his human nature under the immense load of sufferings he endured, and to impart an infinite value to his sufferings and obedience; and thus render them amply sufficient to atone for the sins, and to justify the persons, of all who shall believe in him to the end of time.

Blessed be God, I feel confident that he is able and willing to save unto the uttermost all that will come unto God by him. I therefore come to him, and commit my immortal soul into his hands, and intrust to him the management of my eternal interests; assured that he can keep what I have committed to him till the great and final day. Blessed be God for such a glorious and all sufficient Savior, and for such assured confidence in his power and grace. Amen.

MEDITATION 7

THE INFINITE CONDESCENSION OF THE REDEEMER

In the counsels of eternity the plan of salvation was laid. Then was it seen that no one in the universe could redeem our fallen race but the Son of God. Will he condescend to become mediator between God and his sinful creatures? He did thus condescend. He most willingly engaged to assume the office; and that we might know his feelings in regard to it, he, ages ago, uttered this cheering language: "Sacrifice and offering thou didst not require; mine ears hast thou opened: burnt-offering and sin-offering hast thou not required. Then said I, Lo, I come: in the volume of the book it is written of me; I delight to do thy will, O my God" (Psalm 40:6-8, Hebrews 10:5-7).

How condescending was our Redeemer in giving to our race such early intimation of his coming to redeem the world, by bruising the serpent's head, or destroying the works of the devil, and in suffering himself to be exhibited to the Church as her Savior, by such a variety of types and ceremonies, and so long a train of prophecies and promises, to sustain her faith!

How condescending was it in the Son of God to assume the fashion of a man, when he appeared to Abraham, and permitted that patriarch to plead with him for the preservation of Sodom, that guilty and polluted city (Genesis 18)! As the angel in whom was Jehovah's name, he condescended to conduct the tribes of Israel through the wilderness to the land of promise; he too watched over the interests of his Church, while dwelling in that chosen land; and then in the appointed time, he appeared on this earth, in human form, to accomplish his glorious and gracious work of saving our race!

And while engaged in his work in what various forms was his

condescension displayed!

When Nicodemus, ashamed or afraid to let it be known that he entertained any favorable sentiments towards our Redeemer, came by night to converse with him, he did not sternly rebuke him for his timidity or cowardice, but graciously condescended to enter into conversation with him, to answer his questions, and to impart the most important instructions.

How did his condescension shine in his conversation with the woman of Samaria! Wearied with his journey he sat down on Jacob's well, while his disciples had gone to buy meat in a neighboring city. A woman of Samaria came to the well to draw water; and, to lead her into conversation designed for her spiritual benefit, he asked her to give him drink. As the Jews had no dealings with the Samaritans, she expressed her surprise that he being a Jew, should make such a request. In the prejudices of the Jews, our blessed Lord did not participate. He immediately, by his heavenly conversation, turned her attention to that living water that imparts life to the soul, and pursued his conversation with her, so that she and many of the Samaritans were led to believe him to be the promised Messiah (John 4).

With what condescension did our Lord treat Martha, the sister of Lazarus and Mary! Being of an anxious and fretful disposition, while cumbered with much serving, and desirous of preparing a suitable supper for her guests, she came in a pettish manner to Jesus, and complaining of the conduct of her wise and prudent sister, she without becoming reverence gave utterance to her improper feelings: "Lord, dost thou not care that my sister hath left me to serve alone? Bid her therefore that she help me." To this impertinent application, our Lord meekly replied: "Martha, Martha, thou art careful and troubled about many things; but one thing is needful: and Mary hath chosen that good part, which shall not be taken from her" (Luke 10:40-42).

Such was our Redeemer's attachment to this family, that although the Jews had sought to stone him, yet, to raise Lazarus from the dead, he, to the surprise of his disciples, went to that part of the land; and, with what affectionate condescension toward them, did he act! Seeing Mary weeping, and the Jews also weeping who came with her, "he groaned in spirit, and was troubled." "Jesus wept." Well might the Jews exclaim, "Behold, how he loved him!" Approaching the grave, he said to Martha, whose faith wavered, "Said I not unto thee, that, if thou wouldest believe, thou shouldest see the glory of God?" Then, lifting up his eyes to heaven, he said for the benefit of all present, "Father, I thank thee that thou hast heard me;" and, with a loud voice, he commanded Lazarus to come forth. Lazarus obeyed, came forth, and lived (John 11).

How frequently the Redeemer manifested his condescension toward his disciples in bearing with their infirmities, dullness, and want of faith! What a surprising exhibition of unequalled condescension we see, when, to set them an example of humility and brotherly love, he, knowing that the Father had given all things into his hands, and that he was come from God, and went to God, arose from supper, and laid aside his garments, and took a towel and girded himself; and having poured water into a basin, began to wash the disciples' feet and to wipe them with the towel wherewith he was girded! Behold, the Lord of glory, while conscious of his exalted standing in the universe, stoops to perform such menial acts for the instruction of his disciples!

Peter, when the Redeemer had said to his disciples, "all ye shall be offended because of me this night," made solemn protestations of his unwavering attachment; and yet slept, with James and John, while their Master was agonizing in the garden! How was he treated? Jesus, when he found them sleeping, said unto Peter, "Simon, sleepest thou? Couldst not thou watch one hour? Watch ye and pray, lest ye enter into temptation"; and then kindly adds this apology, "The spirit truly is ready, but the flesh is weak" (Mark 14:27-42). Peter shamefully denied his Lord; and when he had repeated his great offense three times, "the Lord turned, and looked upon Peter." How piercing this look of his suffering Master! Peter's heart felt it. "He went out and wept bitterly" (Luke 22:61-62). All his disciples had failed in duty more or less, yet their merciful Savior, after he had arisen from the dead, received them into favor again, and renewed their commission to the apostleship. What kindness and condescension are seen in all these occurrences! How worthy of all admiration!

Such was the condescension of the Redeemer, both before, and after, his incarnation. And now, while ascended to his Mediatorial throne, and reigning in inconceivable glory as Lord of heaven and earth, is he not as condescending as ever? Does he not love, watch over, and defend his Church? Does he not bear her on his heart, interceding for her before the throne of the Most High?

And hast not thou, my soul, shared in his great condescension and loving-kindness? Whose eye watched over thee, whilst thou wast wandering far from righteousness, forgetful and unconcerned about thy eternal interests? Who laid the restraints of providence and grace upon thee; so as to keep thee from the great sins to which thou wast tempted? Was it not thy condescending Savior, who loved thee, while wandering away from him, heedless of his kind invitations to return and receive his salvation? Who, in the appointed time, sent his Spirit to awaken, to arouse, to convict, and convert thee? Who washed away thy sins, and brought thee into a state of reconciliation and favor with God? Who has kept and guarded thee, healed thy backslidings and quickened thee in the service of God, and brightened thy hopes? Hast thou not received all these signal favors from the loving-kindness of thy condescending Savior? Imitate the condescension of thy exalted Master. Banish from thy heart pride and ambition. Condescend to men of low estate.

PRAYER

I bless thee, O my Redeemer, for thine infinite condescension in assuming the office of Mediator between God and man. I praise thee for the early intimation of thy merciful purpose, given in the first promise, concerning the Seed of the woman who was to bruise the serpent's head, and for the subsequent clearer discoveries afforded by various predictions and promises concerning the Messiah and his work. I bless thee for the proofs of thy willingness to execute the office of Mediator, manifested by appearing to the patriarchs in human form, and thus anticipating the assumption of our nature in the appointed time. I praise thee for condescending to lead, as the Angel of the covenant, the chosen tribes through the wilderness to the land of promise; and for condescending to superintend and manage the affairs of thy church, till thy advent in the world. I bless thee for the condescension displayed in thy public ministry, and in thy treatment of thy disciples, and of all who apply to thee for instructions; and for the condescension so signally shown to thy disciples, after thy resurrection from the dead, by repeated appearances to them, in order to afford to them infallible proofs that thou wast alive again, and about to ascend in glory to heaven.

Infinite condescension! May I be enabled to imbibe thy spirit, and always in my intercourse with my fellow disciples, and with my fellow men, show this lovely trait of character. May I ever be as my Savior was, "meek and lowly in heart;" that thus I may prove myself a true disciple of my blessed Redeemer. Amen.

MEDITATION 8

THE PROFOUND HUMILIATION OF CHRIST

Our blessed Lord has not only displayed infinite condescension, but submitted to the most profound humiliation.

Of his humiliation we find a summary and comprehensive view given by the apostle Paul, in his epistle to the Philippians: "Who, being in the form of God, thought it not robbery to be equal with God: but made himself of no reputation, and took upon him the form of a servant, and was made in the likeness of men: and being found in fashion as a man, he humbled himself, and became obedient unto death, even the death of the cross" (Philippians 2:6-7). Here is exhibited the humiliation of our blessed Lord from its commencement to its termination. It demands an attentive consideration in all its parts. Let me devoutly look at them.

1. He, being in the form of God, was equal with God. As such he was seen by angels: seated on the throne of heaven in all his infinite majesty, demanding and receiving the worship of every order of celestial beings. Before him angels and archangels cast their crowns, and prostrated themselves at his feet, in acknowledgment of his supreme excellence, and of their entire dependence on him for existence and every endowment. "But he made himself of no reputation" (in the original, "he emptied himself"); laid aside his glory; did not make such manifestations of his august majesty as he did to angels, and had done to the patriarchs when he appeared to them, as to Abraham, and to Moses, and to the children of Israel at mount Sinai, when he published the law in such terrific displays of grandeur and majesty.

2. This emptying himself was done by taking upon himself the form of a servant. To this act of humiliation the Son of God consented, by agreeing to become a Mediator; for it involved the assumption of the

nature of that order of creatures for whom he became mediator; and rendered him, who was above all law and authority, and subject to no being whatever, servant to his eternal Father, and subjected him in his assumed nature, to the law that had been given to that nature. Had the Son of God assumed into personal union with himself the highest created nature in the universe, it would have been unspeakable condescension, and would have placed him in the condition of a servant to his eternal Father.

3. He made a lower stoop than this. "He was made in the likeness of men." He did not assume the nature of angels; he did not appear in the likeness of Michael or Gabriel: but he assumed the nature of man, who, although made in the image and likeness or his Creator, yet was inferior to angels. And he assumed this nature not as it was in a state of innocence, free from all the consequences of sin, and all the seeds of disease and death, but as it had become by transgression, subject to many ills, and finally to death. "He was made like unto us in all things, sin only excepted." In this inferior nature, degraded as it was by sin, our blessed Redeemer appeared as a servant to his Father.

4. There is another step in his humiliation; for the apostle says, that, "being found in fashion as a man, he humbled himself, and became obedient." He was pleased to place himself under obligation to obey the law, not only as it governed man in a state of innocence, but as it was presented to him in his fallen state. In token of this obligation, he was, on the eighth day, circumcised; and became subject to the whole Mosaic law, moral, ceremonial, and civil. He observed the Jewish feasts, the temple-service, and paid tribute-money. His obedience was perfect; free from every defect in regard to principle, action, and continuance; and rendered, in circumstances of peculiar difficulty, in opposition to prevailing customs, and the prescriptions of the scribes and rulers; and the most violent assaults of temptations, urged by Satan, in every form,

and with the greatest violence.

5. The Savior rendered himself subject to the law, not only in its preceptive, but in its penal demands. "He became obedient unto death." He was the substitute of man, and engaged to satisfy all the demands of the divine law on fallen man. In his innocent state, the law required from man nothing but obedience to its holy precepts. Had he rendered this, by retaining the purity of his heart and life, the law would have demanded nothing more. He would have been righteous, and entitled to the promised reward. He failed in his obedience; he sinned; and the law obtained a new demand; it required a full satisfaction for the dishonor done to it by disobedience.

To this demand the Savior submitted, and engaged, as man's Redeemer, to pay all his debts, by subjecting himself to all the sufferings which a full satisfaction for sin required.

This part of the Savior's humiliation comprehends all the sufferings which he endured, from the beginning to the close of his life; and will come under review in a subsequent meditation. Let me at present look at that part named by the apostle in the terms "death, even the death of the cross." "As it is appointed unto men once to die," he stooped so low as to endure this evil. His soul was separated from his body; his blessed body became lifeless, and was laid in the grave.

His death was produced, not by disease, nor by the mere hand of violence; but by a judicial act, which condemned him to a death of the most shameful kind; a death inflicted on slaves, thieves, and murderers. It was the death of the cross. And his death on the cross was attended with every circumstance of pain and shame, and violence, that could be combined together by the malice and ingenuity of his malignant enemies.

So profound was the humiliation of the Son of God! The Sovereign of the universe became a servant; the great Creator, a dependent creature; the supreme Lawgiver, a subject to his own law! He, whose palace is the highest heaven, had no dwelling place of his own; he, who issues his orders to the armies of heaven, and is worshiped by angels and archangels, was attended by a few fishermen and publicans; he, who is infinitely rich became poor and dependent on charity for subsistence! He, of whom it is written, "none can stay his hand, or say unto him, What doest thou?" was opposed by Jewish rulers and priests! He, who spake, and soldiers who came to arrest him, fell to the ground, and would have died had he willed it; suffered himself to be bound by them, and led to the high priest. The Judge of all, was judged by the Jewish council; mocked by Herod; scourged, condemned, and crucified by the Roman governor! The Author of life in every form died by the hands of wicked men! The well beloved Son of God agonized under the hidings of his Father's face, and the infliction of the cure of his holy and violated law!

To all this humiliation our blessed Lord submitted for the salvation of his people. How amazing! How frequently should I contemplate it by faith, and endeavor to imbibe the spirit that prompted him to set such an example to his people! True, it was designed for a more important purpose, to make a real expiation for sin; still I may see in it a bright and glorious example, worthy of my devout and affectionate imitation. Immediately before, and in connection with this exhibition of the Savior's humiliation, the apostle says, "Let this mind be in you, which was also in Christ Jesus," and then proceeds to describe this mind of Christ, by showing how it appeared in his profound humiliation.

Dwell then, my soul, on this amazing scene of humiliation and sufferings of thy Lord and Redeemer, to imbibe his spirit of humility and love. Be willing to humble thyself, and suffer too, when necessary for the glory of God, and the good of thy fellow Christians and fellow men. Pray for the grace of the Holy Spirit, to mold thee into the blessed likeness of thy Savior God.

PRAYER

How profound thy humiliation, O my Redeemer God! Hadst thou been pleased to assume the nature of an archangel, it would have claimed the admiration and praise of all holy beings. But, by assuming the nature of fallen man, and appearing in the form of a servant, for our salvation, thou didst submit to humiliation still more profound! I bless thee that thou wast willing to lay aside the robes of Godhead, to take human nature from a humble virgin, to be born in a stable, and laid in a manger. I praise thee for every step in thy humiliation; that thou didst willingly subject thyself to the law of man—to live in poverty—to incur the opposition of the Jewish priests and rulers—to endure reproach and reviling—to stand in judgment at the bar of thy creatures—to submit to condemnation, as if guilty of blasphemy and sedition—and to bear all the agonies and tortures connected with the shameful death of crucifixion, as well as the more overwhelming sufferings inflicted on thy soul by divine justice, in expiation of the sins of thy people!

May I ever remember, with gratitude and praise, this astonishing humiliation; and, imbibing thy spirit, manifest, on all suitable occasions, the same mind that prompted thee, O Savior, to submit to humiliation so profound and wonderful! Amen.

Meditation 9

The Holy Life of Christ

The spotless purity of the Savior was essential to his office and work as Mediator. Had his human nature been defiled by sin, he could not have yielded that perfect obedience which the law demanded; nor would it have received the high honor of being hypostatically united to his divine nature. That his human nature was perfectly pure from every moral stain, the sacred Scriptures bear ample testimony. "Therefore also," said the angel Gabriel to Mary, "that holy thing which shall be born of thee shall be called the Son of God" (Luke 1:35). At his baptism a voice came from heaven, which said, "Thou art my beloved Son; in thee I am well pleased" (Luke 3:22). And again, at his transfiguration, the Father testified his approbation of him: "This is my beloved Son: hear him" (Luke 9:35). Appealing to his enemies, Jesus said, "Which of you convinceth me of sin?" (John 8:46). And the apostle, "For such a high priest became us, who is holy, harmless, undefiled, and separated from sinners, and made higher than the heavens; who needed not, as those high priests, to offer up sacrifice, first for his own sins" (Hebrews 7:26-27).

Jesus was indeed a descendant of Adam; for he was born of the virgin Mary, but not in the ordinary way. He was conceived in the virgin's womb, by the power of the Holy Ghost, and came by a special promise, given after the apostasy of man; and not being represented by Adam in the covenant of works, he was not at all affected by the violation of that covenant, and could not be involved in its consequences.

What matter of gratitude and praise, to be thus divinely assured that Christ was perfectly qualified for the work he undertook! Rejoice, my soul, in this assurance, and let it inspire thee with unshaken confidence in him.

Being perfectly pure in his nature at his birth, our blessed Redeemer remained so through the whole of his course on earth. In heart and life he was perfectly conformed to the divine law. The law, or holiness, was in him personified. It beamed from his eyes, breathed from his lips, and moved in all his actions. The grand comprehensive principles of the law were deeply seated in his holy soul. He loved God with all his powers, and his neighbor as himself; and his whole life was one continued, unbroken stream of love.

His love to his Father was displayed by his steady, uniform, unwavering and perfect obedience to his commandments. "I came down from heaven, not to do mine own will, but the will of him that sent me" (John 6:38). "But that the world may know that I love the Father; and as the Father gave me commandment, even so I do. Arise, let us go hence" (John 14:31). "I have glorified thee on the earth; I have finished the work which thou gavest me to do" (John 7:4).

His obedience to his Father's will was ever characterized by those qualities that render obedience truly acceptable.

Delight was one characteristic. In view of all the difficulties and sufferings to be encountered and endured, he could truly say, "Lo, I come: in the volume of the book it is written of me; I delight to do thy will, O my God" (Psalm 40:7-8).

The obedience of Christ was marked by a *devotional spirit*. He felt his dependence on God and, therefore, conversed much with him by prayer. Before the choice of his apostles, "he went into a mountain to pray, and continued all night in prayer to God" (Luke 6:12-13). And, on another occasion, "rising up a great while before day, he went out, and departed into a solitary place, and there prayed" (Mark 1:35). How earnest were his prayers in the garden of Gethsemane! "Who in the days of his flesh," says the apostle, "when he had offered up prayers and supplications, with strong cries and tears unto Him that was able to save him from death, and was heard in that he feared" (Hebrews 5:7). His heart was continually ascending to God in holy aspirations, and held high communion with him.

How fervent was the Redeemer's *zeal* for his Father's honor! When but twelve years old, he manifested his zeal by remaining at Jerusalem after the departure of his parents, "sitting in the midst of the doctors, both hearing them and asking them questions." And to his mother's question, "Son, why hast thou thus dealt with us? Behold, thy father and I have sought thee sorrowing," he replied, "How is it that ye sought me? Wist ye not that I must be about my Father's business?" (Luke 2:48-49). His zeal was displayed in refuting the corrupt glosses put on the law of God by the Scribes and Pharisees; in condemning the unsound traditions of the elders; and in the heavy denunciations of divine judgments against the false teachers in the Jewish church. And how conspicuous was it, when he purified the temple, by expelling from it all that sold and bought in it (Matthew 21:12-13)! "The zeal of thine house hath eaten me up" (Psalm 69:9; John 2:17).

His *submission* to the divine will was preeminent. How cheerfully did he lead a life of obscurity and poverty! Thrice in the garden, where he agonized, he said, "O my Father, if this cup may not pass away from me, except I drink it, thy will be done" (Matthew 26:39-41).

Trust in God never forsook him. Even in that tremendous hour of overwhelming suffering, when preternatural darkness covered the earth, when all the powers of hell assailed him on the cross, and his Father left him to feel all the horrors of the curse of a broken law, he could still say "*My* God, *my* God, why hast thou forsaken me?" (Matthew 27:46); and closed the awful scene, by crying with a loud voice, "FATHER, into thy hands I commend my spirit" (Luke 23:46).

As the love of Christ to God, so his *benevolence* to *man* was displayed through his whole life. With what diligence did he prosecute his work of teaching. Pressed by the multitudes attending his ministry, he at times could hardly find leisure to eat. When the people were in danger of fainting for want of food, he fed them in a miraculous manner. He bore with the dullness, infirmities and unbelief of his apostles. "He went about doing good" (Acts 10:38). He healed all manner of diseases; rejected none that sought his aid; and welcomed all that applied to him for salvation. He wept at the grave of Lazarus. He pitied his enemies. In view of the miseries that were coming upon the wicked city that had rejected him, how melting the strains of pity he uttered! "O Jerusalem, Jerusalem, thou that killest the prophets, and stonest them which are sent unto thee, how often would I have gathered thy children together, even as a hen gathereth her chickens under her wings, and ye would not!" (Matthew 23:37). For his enemies who crucified him, he prayed, "Father, forgive them; for they know not what they do" (Luke 23:34). And to the penitent thief on the cross, who *had reviled* him, he gave the assurance, "Verily I say unto thee, Today shalt thou be with me in paradise" (Luke 23:43).

May the benevolence of Christ fill my soul, and prompt me to every good deed and act of kindness!

So signal, finished, and sinless was the Savior's obedience to the divine law! The development of his love to God and man so complete and attractive! And in rendering his obedience he rose above every difficulty, triumphed over all opposition, and contemned every adverse allurement. The devil assailed him at the commencement of his public life, with all his cunning and power; but in vain. In vain he spread before him all the kingdoms of the world, and their glory, promising to give them all to him, if he would worship him. "Get thee behind me, Satan," replied the indignant Redeemer: "for it is written, Thou shalt worship the Lord thy God, and him only shalt thou serve" (Luke 4:5-8). The world had no power over him. He was alike superior to its smiles and frowns, to its rewards and terrors. When he saw that the people were disposed to take him by force and make him a king, he retired from them and concealed himself.

The world could crucify, but it could not subdue him. There was a joy set before him, a joy springing from the glory of God, in the redemption of a fallen world, and his own future exaltation, that enabled him to endure the cross and despise its shame (Hebrews 12:2).

What a perfect example I behold in the holy and sinless life of my Redeemer! The lives of patriarchs and pious kings, of holy prophets and apostles, are set before me, that I may copy their examples. They are worthy of my assiduous imitation. Let it, however, be remembered that not one was faultless. But, in the life of my blessed Redeemer, I see an example perfect and faultless. To this, then, my soul, look; and by a reference to it, correct whatever was wrong in the lives of ancient saints and apostles.

PRAYER

Most holy and merciful Savior, when I contemplate the spotless purity of thy nature, and thy perfect and illustrious example, how much reason I find for deep abasement before God, and penitence, on account of the depravity of my nature, and the sins of my life! O! May thy example be ever before my eyes! Afford me grace that I may copy after it. May I imbibe thy spirit and tread in thy steps, and become daily more and more conformed to thy image! O! When shall love to God and man, like thine, possess my whole soul, and control all its feelings, desires, and emotions! and my obedience, flowing from a spring so pure, become what it ought to be, blameless! While passing through this vain and sinful world, may it be my constant prayer and endeavor to walk in that bright path of purity, love, benevolence, and obedience, which thou didst tread, till, at the end of life, being freed from all sin and every stain, I shall become entirely like to thee, my Savior; and see thee as thou art, in all thy purity and infinite glory. Grant this I beseech thee, for thy name's sake. Amen.

MEDITATION 10

THE SUFFERINGS OF THE DEATH OF CHRIST

In preparing for the holy supper, I must especially remember the sufferings and the death of my blessed Lord. It is his broken body and his shed blood he puts into my hands at the sacred feast, and bids me eat the one and drink the other. And can I take the symbols, and thus eat and drink, without remembering what they significantly shadow forth, his amazing sufferings, and bitter and shameful death? No; I must dwell upon this astonishing scene, the sufferings of an incarnate God.

And what were the sufferings of my Redeemer! Ah! What tongue can tell, what mind conceive, what he endured in expiating our sins, and working out our redemption? Divine justice alone can measure them. But let me endeavor to form some conception of their greatness and variety.

They began with his life, and continued till its close. Heaven, earth, and hell combined to afflict him. It pleased his Father to bruise, and to put him to grief, and to make his soul an offering for sin. Devils assailed him with their infernal temptations, especially in the wilderness, and on the cross, to shake his firmness, and to defeat his glorious purpose. Jews and Gentiles united to insult, degrade, and torment him.

He suffered from poverty. He was so poor that he was dependent for subsistence on the charity of others; and to mark the depth of his poverty, he once said, "Foxes have holes, and the birds of the air have nests; but the Son of man hath not where to lay his head" (Matthew 8:20).

He suffered from intercourse with sinful men. Loving God supremely, devoted to his glory, and perfectly free from sin, how painful to his holy soul, must it have been to see the abounding wickedness of men around him; all going astray, all neglecting God, breaking his commandments, and dishonoring, instead of glorifying, his great name! If the soul of righteous Lot was daily vexed with the unlawful deeds of the inhabitants of Sodom, how painful must have been the feelings of the Redeemer, in witnessing the wickedness of the inhabitants of Jerusalem and of Judea!

He suffered from being rejected by the Jews. "He came unto his own; and his own received him not" (John 1:11). By his holy life, by his heavenly doctrines, and by his astonishing miracles, he proved himself to be the long promised Messiah; but his claims were denied by the chief priests, by the Scribes, Pharisees and rulers. They stigmatized him as an impostor, instead of hailing him as their Lord and Redeemer.

He suffered in his reputation. Because he conformed in his living to prevailing custom, he was called a wine bibber and a glutton. Mixing with all classes of men for their instruction, benefit, reformation, and salvation, he was reproached as the friend of publicans and sinners.

He was sold for thirty pieces of silver, and betrayed into the hands of the chief priests, by a kiss from Judas, the traitorous disciple. And now, my soul, behold thy Lord and Savior rudely seized and bound by ruffian soldiers, and led by them to the palace of the high priest. There, with what cruel indignity is he treated! He is mocked, smitten on the face, and spit upon. He is blindfolded, and then asked to tell who smote him. False witnesses testify against him. Adjured by the high priest, he affirms himself to be the Son of God; and immediately the council condemn him as deserving death.

Deprived of the power of executing the sentence of death, they hurry him to Pilate the Roman governor; and before his tribunal, accusing him as a blasphemer, and as a seditious person, demand his death. Pilate sends him to Herod the king. He and his soldiers mock and insult him, and then send him back again to Pilate. Convinced of his innocence, the Roman governor seeks to deliver him. Persuaded by the priests, a fickle people, who had a little before admired Jesus, prefer to him for release Barabbas, a robber and murderer. Pilate overcome by the importunity of the chief priests and the clamorous demands of the multitude, cowardly yields to their wishes.

What a scene now ensues! The blessed Jesus is scourged, and then led by the soldiers into the common hall, and the whole band collected around him to participate in his sufferings. They strip off his own raiment, and put on him a scarlet robe. Having put on his head a plaited crown of thorns, and a reed in his right hand, they bow the knee before him, and mock him, saying, Hail, king of the Jews. They spit upon him; and taking the reed out of his hand, they smite him on the head. Tired with their mockery and insults, they take off the scarlet robe, and put on him his own raiment, and lead him away to crucify him.

Behold him, my soul, walking, with painful steps, to mount Calvary, to be crucified. See him nailed to the cross, and then lifted up on it, that it may be thrust violently into the hole prepared for it; by which shock every joint of his sacred body is dislocated. Behold the innocent Lamb of God between two crucified malefactors, as if the most deserving of death. They that passed by revile him, wagging their heads, and saying, "Thou that destroyest the temple, and buildest it in three days, save thyself. If thou be the Son of God, come down from the cross" (Matthew 27:40). Hear the malignant mocking of the chief priests, the scribes and elders: "He saved others, himself, he cannot save. If he be the King of Israel, let him now come down from the cross, and we will believe him. He trusted in God; let him deliver him now, if he will have him: for he said, I am the Son of God" (Matthew 27:42-43).

These outward insults, these torments inflicted on his body, I am to consider and remember; but especially am I to contemplate what was far more overwhelming, the sorrows of his soul. The former he bore in silence; but the latter drew from him the complaints in the garden, and the bitter cry on the cross.

But how shall I form a conception of the agonies of my Savior's soul, while bearing our sins? In Gethsemane, there was no external cause of pain, no enemy seizing him, no injury done to his body. Yet I see him sore amazed and very heavy, prostrate on the ground, and earnestly pouring out his supplications to his Father, saying "If it be possible, let this cup pass from me," and saying to his disciples, "My soul is exceedingly sorrowful, even unto death: tarry ye here, and watch with me" (Matthew 26:38-39). What produced this mental agony, which was so great as to force the blood through the pores of his skin, falling on the ground? Not the fear of the Jews, not the terror of the Roman sword. At these he did not tremble. He met them with undisturbed self-possession.

What then, my soul, were the causes of this mysterious agony? Ah! It was a sense of the infinite evil of sin, which he was to bear—an apprehension of the wrath of God which he was to feel in his soul—a sight of the fearful curse of the law which was to be poured out upon him. These, and not the fear of what man could inflict on his body, were the causes of his mysterious and overwhelming mental agonies, in the garden of Gethsemane.

This may help me to form some conception of what my Savior endured, during the three hours of preternatural darkness that concealed him from mortal view, while hanging on the cross, and when God emphatically made his SOUL AN OFFERING FOR SIN, by hiding his face from him, withdrawing from him a comforting sense of his approbation and love, and pouring out upon his soul unmingled wrath. It was this that extorted from him the doleful cry, "My God, my God, why hast thou forsaken me?" (Matthew 27:46).

And now recollecting, that my blessed Redeemer, in making expiation for the sins of the world, was enduring in a few hours, sufferings that, measured by divine justice, were to be a full equivalent for the everlasting torments of all who shall be saved, by believing on him, I may form some feeble conception of the immensity of his sufferings, and see that he endured what none but God could inflict, and none but God could sustain.

Having borne all these overwhelming agonies, my Savior said, "It is finished," and yielded up his spirit into the hands of his Father (John 19:30).

He died, was taken down from the cross, was buried, and remained in the grave part of three days.

PRAYER

O my dear Redeemer, didst thou endure all these great and overwhelming sufferings for me! How wonderful thy love! What gratitude! What returns of love are due to thee! How should I be constrained to live for thee, who didst die, and revive, and rise again, that thou mightest be Lord both of the dead and the living! How joyfully should I do any service appointed, and patiently bear any suffering to which thou mayest call me! O for grace thus to act, and thus to suffer!

In the light of thy cross may I see the horrible nature of sin, and hate it with a perfect hatred. Give me to feel the virtue of thy death, that I may die daily unto sin, and live unto righteousness. Thou gavest thyself for us, to redeem us from all iniquity, and purify unto thyself a peculiar people, zealous of good works. Oh! Let thy benevolent and holy design be accomplished in me. Let me be redeemed from all iniquity; and, by thy renewing grace, may I be so quickened as to become zealous of good works. Crucify all my sinful passions and evil propensities; and animate and strengthen every grace and virtue imparted to me by thy Holy Spirit. Hear and grant, O my Savior, these requests, for thy name's sake. Amen.

Meditation 11

The Evil of Sin

Nowhere is the infinite evil of sin seen so clearly and impressively, as in the light of the Redeemer's cross. There its hateful nature and ill-desert are displayed by the most convincing evidence.

By reflecting on the infinite Majesty of the Lawgiver, who is insulted by sin, and considering the excellence of the law, which it violates, its evil clearly appears. The law is good; it corresponds with the relations we sustain; it was designed to promote our happiness; and obedience to its requirements is enforced by infinite authority, and by awful sanctions: so that the violation of it involves the most daring presumption and basest ingratitude, as well as the most foolish disregard to our own happiness.

Its ruinous nature soon became apparent. No sooner had our first parents eaten of the forbidden fruit, than the degrading passion of shame began to work in their bosoms. They saw their nakedness, and made aprons of fig leaves sewed together, to hide it from their eyes. The voice of God had before been music to their ears, and they rejoiced to meet Him; but now, feeling the guilt of sin, they trembled at the sound of that voice, and vainly tried "to hide themselves from the presence of the Lord God among the trees of the garden" (Genesis 3:8).

Arraigned before the bar of their offended Creator, sentence of death is pronounced on the guilty pair. The sorrows of the woman are multiplied; the ground is cursed; man must eat its fruits in sorrow, and in the sweat of his brow, till he return to his native dust. They are expelled from the garden of Eden; and man is doomed to till the ground, now rendered sterile by the curse. Such were the immediate consequences of sin!

How soon the destructive nature of sin appeared! Cain, prompted by this malignant evil, rose up against his righteous brother, who loved him and had done him no harm, and slew him; because God was pleased to show him tokens of his favor, which were withheld from Cain, on account of his disobedience in not complying with the prescribed worship. As men multiplied on the face of the earth, wickedness increased, and the evil nature of sin became more sadly apparent in divisions, contentions, strife, war, and bloodshed; so that God was provoked to express his abhorrence of it, by sweeping away the whole human race from the face of the earth, by a universal deluge; sparing only one family to reproduce the species, and re-people the earth with inhabitants.

The great folly of sin may be seen in the conduct of Noah's descendants, who, to prevent their dispersion over the earth, resolved to build a city and a tower whose top was to reach unto heaven. How vain the design! God had purposed their dispersion; and, to counteract their design, he confounded their language; so that they only who spake the same language could understand each other. Thus were they compelled to desist from their enterprise, and to separate into distinct bodies, and dwell in different regions.

How degrading and polluting sin is seen to be in the beastly and unnatural practices of the people of Sodom; and God's abhorrence of it in the fire that was sent down from heaven upon that guilty city, and its neighbor city, Gomorrah, to consume them on account of their great wickedness!

The history of innumerable wars that have occurred between different tribes and nations of men; the desolation of fruitful fields, the burning of towns and cities, the murdering of their inhabitants; prevailing famines and pestilences; and the torrents of human blood that have been shed, all proclaim the destructive nature of sin, and the wrath of God against it. The vast variety of diseases, and the torturing nature of some, to which humanity is subject, attest to the evil of sin, which has given them birth.

The reign of death, that king of terrors, who has swept away from the earth all past generations of men, is sweeping away this generation, and will sweep away all succeeding generations, till the end of the world, is a standing evidence of the exceeding evil and ill-desert of sin; for his scepter was received from sin, and his destructive empire, founded on man's apostasy from his God.

I stand at the mouth of the tomb. I think of the innumerable millions of the human race who lie down in the mansions of the dead; all reduced to dust and ashes, to one common ruin. I anticipate the day of judgment. I see all who forgot God arraigned before his awful tribunal, trembling at his frowns and expected sentence of condemnation. I hear the terrible words, "Depart from me, ye cursed, into everlasting fire, prepared for the devil and his angels." I see them sinking down to the prison of hell, and plunging into the lake that burneth with fire and brimstone, to be tormented for ever and ever. What a frightful evil is sin, which has caused all this ruin and misery!

But, when I turn to the cross, and behold an incarnate God, bleeding, suffering, agonizing, and dying for the sins of his rebellious creatures, I gain a more impressive view of the horrible evil of sin. Elsewhere I see the creature suffering; but here I see the Creator, in human nature, suffering. There God pours out his wrath upon rebellious men, upon his enemies; here he pours out his wrath upon his innocent and well beloved Son. What impenitent sinner, who looks at this amazing spectacle, can hope to escape merited punishment? How detestable is sin! How should it be shunned as the greatest of all evils!

But, O my soul, when I consider that my Savior suffered for me; that his sacred head was crowned with thorns, his body scourged; his hands and feet torn with rugged nails; his side pierced with the soldier's spear; and his holy soul consumed in the fires of divine justice for my sins, how should I hate these murderers of my Lord! How should my heart break and melt into penitence and love!

Let me keep near to the cross that I may feel its purifying influence. There I find that fountain opened for sin and all uncleanness. There may I wash my soul in the Savior's blood, to cleanse me both from the guilt and pollution of sin. He "gave himself for us, that he might redeem us from all iniquity, and purify unto himself a peculiar people, zealous of good works" (Titus 2:14). With the apostle I may say, "I am crucified with Christ" (Galatians 2:20). United to him I have an interest in his death and in all its benefits. He died for me, that I might die unto sin, and live unto God. Let me then seek to feel both the moral and spiritual influence that issues from my Redeemer's cross. From that sacred source, may I derive the strongest motives to hate sin, and seek holiness. Did he suffer so much on account of my sins? Then must I hate them and crucify them. Has he bought salvation for me? Then what gratitude do I owe to him, and how should it constrain me to live to him who died for me? Did he love me, so as to give himself to the death of the cross? How then should I love him, and give myself to him; by yielding my body a living sacrifice, holy, and acceptable unto God, which is my reasonable service; and my soul, by being transformed by the renewing of my mind, that I may prove what is that good, and acceptable and perfect will of God (Romans 12:1-2)!

And from the cross let me derive a *spiritual* influence to impart vitality, vigor and efficiency to all my motives. The Holy Spirit comes to man in consequence of the death of Christ; and to honor his death, when glorified, he was shed down in so large a measure on the day of Pentecost. Let me, then, seek from my crucified Lord and Savior the gift of the Holy Spirit, to carry on that gracious work, which, I trust, he has begun in my heart. Let me pray for him, as my teacher, my sanctifier, my comforter; and as the Spirit of adoption, to bear witness with my spirit, that I am a child of God, and to seal me unto the day of redemption. Under his blessed influence I shall grow in grace, in piety, and in meetness for heaven.

PRAYER

Gracious God, grant thy blessing to this meditation on the evil of sin. Fill my soul with a growing hatred of it, and grant that I may feel more and more the influence of the Redeemer's cross, in crucifying my sins, and delivering me from their power. Make me holy, as thou art holy, that I may see thee in thy kingdom above. I beseech thee to hear me, for Christ's sake. Amen.

MEDITATION 12

THE RESURRECTION OF CHRIST

The Resurrection of our Lord and Savior is an essential article of the Christian faith. It was as necessary to our justification, as his death was to atone for our sins. Speaking of him the apostle says, "who was delivered for our offenses, and was raised again for our justification" (Romans 4:25). Had he not risen, it would have proved his work to be incomplete; and our salvation would have failed.

The truth of his claims to be the Son of God he himself placed upon his rising from the dead. "What sign showest thou unto us," said the Jews, "seeing that thou doest these things? Jesus answered and said unto them, Destroy this temple, and in three days I will raise it up. But he spake of the temple of his body" (John 2:18-21). His resurrection then was conclusive proof that he was, what he claimed to be, the Son of God, the promised Messiah, and the Savior of the world. Had he been an impostor he certainly could not have raised himself from the dead; nor would God have raised him to life again, and lent the seal of heaven to confirm an imposition on the world. By his resurrection from the dead he was declared to be the Son of God with power (Romans 1:4).

The importance of this article of our faith, the apostle Paul has clearly set forth. "Now if Christ be preached that he rose from the dead, how say some among you that there is no resurrection from the dead? But if there be no resurrection of the dead, then is not Christ risen: and if Christ be not risen, then is our preaching vain, and your faith is also vain. Yea, and we are found false witnesses of God; because we have testified of God that he raised up Christ, whom he raised not up, if so be that the dead rise not. For if the dead rise not, then is not Christ raised: and if Christ be not raised, your faith is vain; ye are yet in your sins. Then they also which are fallen asleep in Christ are perished. If in this life only we have hope in Christ, we are of all men most miserable. But now is Christ risen from the dead, and become the first fruits of them that slept. For since by man came death, by man came also the resurrection of the dead. For as in Adam all die, even so in Christ shall all be made alive. But every man in his own order: Christ the first fruits; afterward they that are Christ's at his coming" (1 Corinthians 15:12-23).

How thankful should we be, that such abundant evidence is afforded to establish our faith in this fundamental article of our holy religion! This great fact, the resurrection of Jesus Christ, was everywhere proclaimed by the apostles. It was so interwoven with the gospel, and lay so at the foundation of our hopes, that it was impossible to preach the gospel, without affirming the Savior's resurrection from the dead. And had we no other evidence of the fact, than the uniform and constant testimony of twelve apostles, it would be sufficient to establish our faith in this great and fundamental truth; for they were commissioned by God to preach, and they proved their commission, by numerous and indubitable miracles, which they wrought in the name of Jesus Christ.

But, in addition to their testimony, we are told how they became convinced that their Lord and Master was alive from the dead. The evidence of the fact presented to them was perfect and infallible. The Redeemer appeared to them, after his resurrection, at sundry times, and in different ways; so that they had afforded to them every method for identifying his risen body with the body in which he had lived, and had been crucified, while on the earth. They saw him; they heard him speak; they conversed with him; they ate with him; they saw the prints of the nails in his hands and feet, and beheld in his side where he had been pierced with the soldier's spear. The evidence presented was irresistible. They all became convinced that their Lord and Master was indeed risen from the dead. Every doubt was expelled from their minds. And of the sincerity of their conviction and belief of this great fact, they gave to the world indubitable evidence, by testifying to the fact in the face of all opposition, reproach, threatenings, persecution, imprisonment, and sufferings; and, finally, by sealing their testimony with their blood.

What testimony can equal this? The witnesses were competent, credible, and numerous. The matter of their testimony was the truth of a fact, presented to their senses; which they had repeated opportunities for examining in the most deliberate manner. They could not be deceived or mistaken in their own belief; and they have given the most ample proof that, in delivering their testimony to the world, they aimed at the glory of God, and the salvation of men.

What an evidence of his resurrection was presented by our Lord on the day of Pentecost! Behold, the Spirit descends from heaven, and fiery cloven tongues are seen, upon the heads of his disciples. They are filled with the Holy Ghost, and begin to speak with other tongues, as the Spirit gives them utterance. What a sudden change is wrought in the apostles! With what boldness are they inspired! They had concealed themselves before, but now they speak publicly with the utmost boldness; testifying the resurrection of Jesus Christ, and charging upon the Jews the crime of having crucified and slain him! How powerful their preaching! Three thousand are converted, and added by baptism to the church, on that memorable day!

And what a conclusive proof of this great fact is seen in the conversion of Saul of Tarsus! He was a bitter persecutor of the church, and a most determined enemy of Jesus Christ. Not satisfied with the evils he had brought on the saints at Jerusalem, he determines to extend his ravages to strange cities. Commissioned by the high priest, he goes to Damascus to persecute them there; and while on the road, "breathing out threatenings and slaughter against the disciples of the Lord" (Acts 9:1), he is prostrated to the ground, by a light from heaven thrown around him, brighter than the noon-day sun. Such overpowering evidence is impressed on his mind, that he becomes convinced at once that he who speaks to him from heaven, is Jesus Christ, whom he was persecuting. He is in a few days converted and baptized. He begins to preach Jesus Christ as the Savior of the world, and the Lord of glory. And ever after he labors in his service with ardent love, untiring zeal, and unshaken constancy; and then offers himself as a sacrifice to his Lord, who loved him, and gave himself for him.

With what confidence may I rest in the assured faith, that my Lord and Redeemer, who was crucified for my sins, arose from the dead on the third day; and in seeing the seal of heaven thus set to the perfection of his great work, as Mediator between God and man! If I am crucified with him, let me rise with him; let me die to sin, as he died for sin; and rise to newnesss of life, as he arose from death to life. Let me live under the influence both of his death and of his life. And as he arose and triumphed over death, as the Head of his church, and as the first fruits of his people, let me rejoice in the pledge thus given, that my body and the bodies of all his people shall be raised in glory hereafter, fashioned like to his most glorious body.

PRAYER

My blessed Redeemer, I rejoice that, on the third day after thy crucifixion, thou didst arise from the dead. I bless thee for appearing so frequently to thy disciples, that they might know thee to be the same person, with whom they had lived and conversed, and from whom they had received so many acts of kindness; and thus be assured, by infallible proofs, that thou wast alive from the dead. I bless thee for the wonders of the day of Pentecost, by which thine apostles were prepared to bear testimony to thy glorious resurrection from the dead, both by their preaching, and by the innumerable miracles which they wrought in thy name. I praise thee, that, by establishing and preserving thy church on the earth, in the midst of the fires of persecution and the rage of devils, thou hast, in every age, given proof of thy resurrection and glorious exaltation to God's right hand.

My Lord and my God, I believe that thou didst arise from the dead, and art alive for evermore. By this wonderful event, by taking up thy life which thou wast pleased to lay down, thou hast firmly established thy claims to Messiahship, and proved thyself to be the Son of God. And God, by raising thee from the dead, has published to the world that thou hast accomplished the mighty work of redemption, and that he is well pleased with it.

And hast thou not, by the work of grace wrought in my heart, given me personal proofs of thy resurrection from the dead? I live because thou livest. Thou art the living vine, from which I derive all my vitality and fruitfulness. Thou livest in me; and "the life that I live, I live by the faith of the Son of God, who loved me and gave himself for me."

I rejoice that thou didst arise as the first fruits of them that sleep, and that hereafter thou wilt raise from the dead my dead body, and the dead bodies of all thy saints; and that thou wilt change our vile bodies, and fashion them like to thy most glorious body, and that we shall live and reign with thee forever in glory.

May I ever feel the power of thy resurrection, and live by faith on this glorious truth of our divine religion. Amen.

MEDITATION 13

CHRIST'S ASCENSION INTO HEAVEN, AND INTERCESSION AT GOD'S RIGHT HAND

Forty days elapsed after his resurrection, before our Redeemer ascended to heaven. During that time he frequently appeared to his disciples to convince them, that he was indeed alive again, conversing with, and instructing them in, things pertaining to the kingdom he was about to set up in the world.

On the fortieth day, the Redeemer, being with his disciples at Jerusalem, commanded them to remain there, till they received the fulfillment of his promise to give them the Holy Ghost, to qualify them for their apostolical ministry. Then leading them out to mount Olivet, "while they beheld, he was taken up" (Acts 1:9). As they gazed at their ascending Lord, with wonder and delight, a cloud intervening concealed him from their view; and two angels appeared, who assured them, that Jesus their Lord, who had left them by ascending to heaven, would hereafter be seen again coming from heaven to judge the world, and complete the salvation of his church. The apostles returned to Jerusalem; and waited there, in obedience to their Master's direction, for the promised gift of the Spirit.

What followed after the cloud had intercepted the apostles' view of their ascending Lord, we are not told. With what speed he moved; by what worlds he passed in going to the highest heavens, we are wholly ignorant. But, from the language of prophecy (Psalm 68:17-18) we may conclude, that angels, who have always taken so deep an interest in the work of redemption, and who were commanded to worship the Son of God, when he was brought into the world (Hebrews 1:6), assembled in great multitudes to form a splendid retinue, and grace the triumphant course of the great Conqueror of sin and the world, of death and hell;

who was now displaying to worlds his triumph, especially over those principalities and powers, who were so eager for his death (Colossians 2:15).

And when the Redeemer, as a conqueror, who had achieved such signal victories, brought such glory to God, and effected salvation for vast numbers of fallen and intelligent creatures, returning to heaven, to receive his promised reward, was approaching the gates of the highest heavens; what a movement must have occurred among all orders of celestial beings! And with what eager delight did they hasten to welcome him to his native home, and pay him the greatest possible honors! (See Psalm 24:7-10.) "Worship him, all ye gods" (Psalm 97:7). "And let all the angels of God worship him" (Hebrews 1:6).

Having entered into heaven, the Redeemer took his seat at the right hand of God. This we are taught to believe: "So then, after the Lord had spoken unto them, he was received up into heaven, and sat on the right hand of God" (Mark 16:19). "Who being the brightness of his glory, and the express image of his person, and upholding all things by the word of his power, when he had by himself purged our sins, sat down on the right hand of the Majesty on high" (Hebrews 1:3).

The import of this phrase may be learned from the following passages of holy Scripture, which speak of the exaltation of Jesus Christ. Paul says, "which he wrought in Christ, when he raised him from the dead, and set him at his right hand in the heavenly places, far above all principality and power, and might, and dominion, and every name that is named, not only in this world, but also in that which is to come: and hath put all things under his feet, and gave him to be head over all things to the church; which is his body, the fullness of him that filleth all in all" (Ephesians 1:20-23). And again he says, "Wherefore God also hath highly exalted him, and given him a name which is above every name: that at the name of Jesus every knee should bow, of things in heaven, and things in earth, and things under the earth; and that every tongue should confess that Jesus Christ is Lord to the glory of God the Father" (Philippians 2:9-11).

The Redeemer, then, is exalted to the highest honor and glory, invested with unlimited dominion over all worlds, and all their inhabitants. Everything, throughout the universe of God, is subjected to his authority and control; and all intelligent creatures of every order are required to worship and obey him. He rules over all; and he will judge all, in the last day; distributing rewards to the righteous, and punishments to the wicked. All this glory and dominion have been conferred upon him, let it be remembered, not as God; for as such he could receive nothing, because he, by his nature, of necessity possessed all things by right of creation: but as man and mediator; in which respect, as he was humbled, so he could be exalted; and being a divine person, he was capable of holding the reins of universal dominion, and conducting the government of the universe with consummate skill and infinite wisdom.

The ascension and exaltation of Jesus Christ our Redeemer, is matter of praise and joy for different reasons. He has received the reward that was promised him when he undertook the mighty work he so nobly accomplished. "For the joy that was set before him, (the joy of glorifying God in the salvation of a lost world), he endured the cross, despising the shame, and is set down on the right hand of the throne of God" (Hebrews 11:2). Who that loves the Savior will not rejoice, that he has received his promised reward, and that this world and all other worlds are governed by him, who loved sinners and gave himself for them? "The Lord," the Savior, "reigneth: let the earth rejoice; let the multitude of isles be glad thereof" (Psalm 97:1).

Another reason for joy, thanksgiving, and praise, is this. The Redeemer has entered heaven as our forerunner (Hebrews 6:19-20); and gone to prepare for his people mansions in his Father's house; to which, in due time, he will receive them, that where he is, there they may be also (John 14:1-3). Being united to Christ by faith, believers have virtually risen and ascended with him, and now sit with him in heavenly places (Ephesians 2:6-7). And does not this demand our praise and thanksgiving to God? and should we not rejoice that our exalted Redeemer holds in his hands our future and eternal inheritance, which he purchased with his precious blood? Behold, my soul, on the throne of the universe, thy Savior, thy Forerunner, thy elder Brother, and thy dearest Friend. Let this furnish thee with a song of thanksgiving, joy, and praise, in the house of thy pilgrimage. "Seek those things that are above, where Christ sitteth at the right hand of God. Set thy affections on things above, not on things on the earth." Thy "life," remember, "is hid with Christ in God" (Colossians 3:1-3). Abide, therefore, in him, and he in thee; and thus thou wilt bring forth much fruit to the glory of God (John 14:5).

The church is safe in the hands of her exalted Head. She is indeed environed with numerous and powerful enemies. But her glorious Redeemer, who loves her, is mighty to save. He triumphed over them on his cross; for by dying he destroyed death and him that had the power of death, that is, the devil. By his death he subverted the empire of Satan, and laid the foundation of his own kingdom that will last forever. His church has been protected and delivered by him in past ages; and he will protect and deliver her in all time to come. Her enemies conquered are held by him in chains as captives. No assault can be made by them without his knowledge and permission; and he will assuredly watch all their designs, and overrule them for the benefit of his people, and finally secure to them a complete victory over them, and cause them to share in his triumph over all his and their enemies.

Rejoice, my soul, that thou art in the hands of One who is mighty to save, and who has said, "My sheep hear my voice, and I know them, and they follow me: and I give unto them eternal life; and they shall never perish, neither shall any pluck them out of my hand. My Father, which gave them me, is greater than all; and no man (no one) is able to pluck them out of my Father's hand. I and my Father are one" (John 10:27-30).

PRAYER

Thou, O my Redeemer, hast "ascended up on high," thou hast "led captivity captive;" thou art seated on the right hand of God; thou art invested with universal dominion. I believe the truth, and rejoice in it. I rejoice that thou hast received the promised reward, and that thou hast gone into heaven as the forerunner of thy people to prepare mansions of rest for them. Thou hast received gifts for men, and thou art bestowing them on thy church. She is safe in thy hand, and no weapon formed against her shall prosper.

And being united to thee by faith, do I not participate with thee in thy ascension and exaltation? Do I not sit with thee in heavenly places? What an influence, then, should this blessed truth have upon me! How should I seek the things that are above, where thou sittest at the right hand of God! O for a heavenly mind! O for a heart to rise above the world, and dwell in heavenly things! Draw me, O my exalted Redeemer, and help me to live in a manner correspondent to my glorious destiny. Prepare me to sit with thee, on thy throne, and to enjoy and praise thee for ever and ever. Amen.

MEDITATION 14

THE INTERCESSION OF CHRIST

Of the Intercession of our great High Priest, was exhibited to the Jewish church an eminent type on the annual day of atonement. On that day their high priest, having offered the prescribed sacrifice, first, for himself, and then for the sins of the people, went into the most holy place, to burn incense and make intercession for the people. So our great High Priest, having offered his prescribed sacrifice, went into heaven, typified by the most holy place in the temple, and made intercession for his church.

But let me mark the difference between the type and the Antitype. The Jewish high priest offered sacrifice for his own sins; but our High Priest, being perfectly free from all personal sins, offered no sacrifice for himself. The former offered animal sacrifices; but the latter offered up Himself as a sacrifice for his people. The sacrifices which the former offered could not take away sin; but the great sacrifice which the latter offered effectually cleanseth from all sin (Hebrews 19:12-14). The former had to offer annually his appointed sacrifices (Hebrews 9:25); but the latter completed his work, by offering his one great sacrifice (Hebrews 9:25-28). The former had to yield his office to his successor (Hebrews 7:28); but the latter, having an unchangeable priesthood, ever liveth to make intercession for his church (Hebrews 7:24-25).

The Redeemer's sacrifice was, in its intrinsic value, sufficient for the salvation of all men; and his ministers are authorized to preach the gospel to all men, and to say to everyone who hears them, "Believe on the Lord Jesus Christ, and thou shalt be saved" (Acts 16:31). But he intercedes in heaven only for his chosen people. So he tells us in that solemn intercessory prayer, which he offered to his Father, just before his crucifixion. "I pray for them: I pray not for the world, but for them which thou hast given me;

for they are thine. And all mine are thine and thine are mine; and I am glorified in them. Neither pray I for these alone, but for them also which shall believe on me through their word" (John 17:9-10, 20).

Every believer may rest assured, that *his name* is written on the heart of our great High Priest, and that he intercedes for him before the throne.

How invaluable the blessings for which our glorious Intercessor prays! He does not ask that we should be taken out of the world, but that we should be kept from the evil. He is willing that we should be left in the world, evil and ensnaring as it is, to accomplish our assigned work, in the allotted time; but he prays to his Father, that we may be kept from the evil One, and not permitted to be overcome by his subtle and wicked devices, and may be sanctified more and more, by the purifying influence of the word of God.

Another blessing for which he prays, is one that claims the serious consideration of all professing Christians. It is their unity: "That they may be one, even as we are one; I in them, and thou in me, that they may be made perfect in one; that the world may know that thou hast sent me, and hast loved them, as thou hast loved me" (John 17:22-23). Does our blessed Redeemer pray to his Father that his disciples may love one another, and exhibit such unity, as will convince the world, that they are animated by principles which the world does not possess, and bring honor to their heavenly source; and shall we not endeavor to cultivate the kindest feelings of brotherly love; avoiding all strife and contentions, that would mar and obscure our unity of spirit and heart?

Nor is this all: our blessed Lord prays for the consummation of the happiness of his disciples in the kingdom of his glory. He leaves them, for an appointed time, in the world, to endure afflictions and trials, and to serve God in their day and generation; but he designs them for a higher and a heavenly state of existence, near to himself, the Lord of glory. Of this we are assured in his solemn intercessory prayer: "Father, I will that they also, whom thou hast given me, be with me where I am; that they may behold my glory, which thou hast given me: for thou lovedst me before the foundation of the world" (John 17:24).

How prevailing the intercession of our great High Priest! He pleads for us, not like one supplicating for blessings, which he knows he does not deserve; but, as a Son with his Father, who knows he prays for promised blessings, which were purchased with his blood. His intercession, founded on his all meritorious sacrifice, must be ever prevailing. At the grave of Lazarus, he said, "Father, I thank thee, that thou hast heard me. And I knew that thou hearest me always: but because of the people that stand by I said it, that they may believe that than hast sent me" (John 11:41-42). Not one for whom he intercedes shall fail of salvation; not one petition he presents can fail to be heard and granted.

Is a doubt excited in the mind, by the want of unity in the church? Will anyone inquire, how the discordant state of Christendom accords with the prayer of our Savior for the unity of his disciples? They are united in the strictest manner; living in union to one Lord—under the same government—inhabited by one Spirit—rejoicing in the same blessed hope—children of the same heavenly family—meeting daily at the same throne of grace—heirs of the same kingdom, and animated by the same love for Christ, for his cause, and people. In primitive times their love for each other was so conspicuous, as to attract and command the admiration of the heathen; and hereafter Christian love will so burn as to consume all obstructions to its heavenly course, and make the church *visibly*, as she always has been *spiritually, one blessed society*. The apparent want of union arises from the great number of mere professors, who have attached themselves to the visible church, and the corrupting and disorganizing influence of civil governments in her affairs.

Welcome that happy period, when all these obstructions to the visible unity of the church, shall be removed; when political men shall keep within their appropriate sphere, and leave her government to those to whose hands her glorious Head has committed it: and when all her members shall be what they profess to be! Then shall the world be indeed convinced of the divine mission of Jesus Christ; and the church on earth be a beautiful and glorious type of the church in heaven; where the prevailing influence of our great Intercessor, will be seen, in all its glorious power, without an intervening cloud to obscure the most perfect unity of all his redeemed people.

Love to Christ and love to one another, will bind them together in the closest and most intimate unity, free from every discordant feeling, forever, to the glory of God and of the Lamb. O! Blessed consummation of grace, and love, and glory, come quickly, and let the Redeemer see of the travail of his soul, and be satisfied!

PRAYER

Most High and Holy God, by the intercession of our great High Priest, I am reminded of my fallen and sinful condition. Man, while innocent and holy, stood in no need of a mediator. He had immediate access, like the holy angels, to thy throne, and could offer up his prayers, thanksgivings, and praises acceptably to his Creator and Benefactor. But this great privilege he has forfeited by sin. Guilty and depraved, it does not become infinite purity to allow him to approach for worship, but through a Mediator. Blessed be thy great name, we have a glorious Mediator, who has opened up for us a new and living way of access to the mercy-seat, through the rent veil, that is, his flesh. In infinite mercy thine own Son has been appointed to this high office; who, having offered up himself as a sacrifice for sin, has gone as our High Priest into heaven, the most holy place, to intercede for his people. And blessed be thy name, we have now the privilege of drawing nigh by him into thy presence, with boldness, and to ask of thee, with believing confidence, every needed blessing.

Gracious God, grant me faith in this great High Priest and Intercessor. O! May my worthless name be graven on his heart, and I be an object of his prevailing intercession. Let all the blessings for which he prays be bestowed on me. May I be preserved from the evil one, kept, and guarded and preserved by thy power and grace, while I remain in this world! Sanctify me by thy truth; and grant, I beseech thee, that I may be enabled to keep the unity of the Spirit in the bond of peace. May I cherish and cultivate the kindest feelings of brotherly love towards my fellow disciples, and, at last, be taken to Christ, to dwell with him, and behold his glory. Hear my prayer, and grant all these blessings, I beseech thee, O Lord, my God, for the sake of my great High Priest and Advocate, Jesus Christ. Amen.

Meditation 15

Christ Coming to Judgment

Of this sublime event we are reminded by the words of our Lord in his precious institution: "For as often as ye eat this bread, and drink this cup, ye do show the Lord's death till he come" (1 Corinthians 11:26).

Like the Passover, the Lord's supper has a double aspect. As the former looked back to the deliverance of Israel from Egyptian bondage, and forward to that greater deliverance of the true Israel from bondage to sin, the world and Satan, which it typified; so the Lord's supper looks back to the accomplishment of our redemption by his great sacrifice, and forward to his second coming to complete our salvation.

That God will, at some future day, judge the world, human reason can infer from the disorder prevailing in the present state of things. It cannot be that under the government of righteousness, the wicked should oppress the good, without being called to an account for their evil deeds. Vice may triumph for a time over virtue; but its triumph will be short. The honor of God's righteousness requires that the prevalent disorder in human affairs, should be corrected, and that the world should learn, that he will appear as the friend of righteousness, and as the enemy of unrighteousness.

But we are not left to our reason to establish this great truth, so important to be known. In every age, God has, by his inspired prophets, assured mankind, that he will summon them before his awful and righteous tribunal, to render up to him an account of their conduct in the present state, and to receive their rewards and punishments. "Enoch, the seventh from Adam, prophesied of these things, saying, Behold, the Lord cometh with ten thousand of his saints, to execute judgment upon all, and to convince all that are ungodly among them of all their ungodly deeds, which they have ungodly committed, and of all their hard speeches which ungodly sinners have spoken against him" (Jude 14-15). David proclaims this great truth: "Our God shall come, and shall not keep silence: a fire goeth before him, and it shall be very tempestuous round about him. He shall call to the heavens from above, and to the earth that he may judge his people. Gather my saints together unto me; those that have made a covenant with me by sacrifice. And the heavens shall declare his righteousness: for God is judge himself" (Psalm 50:3-6). Paul reasoned of "righteousness, of temperance, and judgment to come, and Felix trembled" (Acts 24:25). And in his epistle to the Hebrews he affirms, "It is appointed unto men once to die, but after this the judgment" (Hebrews 9:27). John says "I saw a great white throne, and him that sat on it, from whose face the earth and the heaven fled away: and there was found no place for them. And I saw the dead, small and great, stand before God; and the books were opened: and another book was opened, which is the book of life: and the dead were judged out of those things which were written in the books, according to their works. And the sea gave up the dead which were in it; and death and hell delivered up the dead which were in them: and they were judged every man, according to their works" (Revelation 20:11-13).

The day of judgment is fixed; "but of that day and that hour knoweth no man, no not the angels which are in heaven, but my Father only" (Matthew 24:36). Hence it is written, "The day of the Lord so cometh as a thief in the night" (2 Peter 3:10).

Awful day! "But the heavens and the earth, which are now, by the same word, are kept in store, reserved unto fire against the day of judgment and perdition of ungodly men; in the which the heavens shall pass away with a great noise, and the elements shall melt with fervent heat, the earth also and the works that are therein shall be burned up" (2 Peter 3:7, 10).

But let me rejoice, the Judge, before whose bar I shall be arraigned, and from whose lips I shall hear the sentence that will determine my everlasting condition, is the Lord Jesus. So he assures me. "The Father judgeth no man, but hath committed all judgment unto the Son, that all men should honor the Son, even as they honor the Father. He that honoreth not the Son, honoreth not the Father which hath sent him. Verily, verily, I say unto you, He that heareth my word, and believeth on him that sent me, hath everlasting life, and shall not come into condemnation; but is passed from death unto life. Verily, verily, I say unto you, The hour is coming, and now is, when the dead shall hear the voice of the Son of God: and they that hear shall live. For as the Father hath life in himself, so hath he given to the Son to have life in himself; and hath given him authority to execute judgment also, because he is the Son of man. Marvel not at this: for the hour is coming, in the which all that are in the graves shall hear his voice, and shall come forth: they that have done good unto the resurrection of life; and they that have done evil, unto the resurrection damnation" (John 5:22-29).

How exalted and glorious will my Savior then appear to an assembled universe! "When the Son of man shall come in his glory, and all the holy angels with him, then shall he sit upon the throne of his glory: and before him shall be gathered all nations: and he shall separate them one from another, as a shepherd divideth his sheep from the goats: and he shall set the sheep on his right hand, but the goats on the left. Then shall the King say unto them on his right hand, Come, ye blessed of my Father, inherit the kingdom prepared for you from the foundation of the world; for I was an hungered, and ye gave me meat; I was thirsty, and ye gave me drink: I was a stranger, and ye took me in; naked, and ye clothed me: I was sick, and ye visited me: I was in prison, and ye came unto me." Oh! The infinite condescension and mercy of the Redeemer, thus to notice and reward the good deeds done by his disciples, to their fellow disciples, as if done to himself! "And then shall he say unto them on the left hand, Depart from me, ye cursed into everlasting fire, prepared for the devil and his angels: for I was hungered, and ye gave me no meat: I was thirsty, and ye gave me no drink: I was a stranger, and ye took me not in: naked, and ye clothed me not: sick and in prison, and ye visited me not" (Matthew 25:31-43).

How terrible will be that day of glory to his enemies; "when the Lord Jesus shall be revealed from heaven, with his mighty angels, in flaming fire, taking vengeance on them that know not God, and obey not the gospel of our Lord Jesus Christ: who shall be punished with everlasting destruction from the presence of the Lord and from the glory of his power" (2 Thessalonians 1:7-9). But how joyful will it be to his friends, "when he shall come to be glorified in his saints, and admired in all them that believe" (verse 10). "For the Lord himself shall descend from heaven with a shout, with the voice of the archangel, and with the trump of God: and the dead in Christ shall rise first" (1 Thessalonians 4:16). "Behold, I show you a mystery. We shall not all sleep, but we shall all be changed. In a moment, in the twinkling of an eye, at the last trump; for the trumpet shall sound, and the dead shall be raised incorruptible, and we shall be changed. For this corruptible must put on incorruption, and this mortal must put on immortality. So then when this corruptible shall have put on incorruption, and this mortal shall have put on immortality, then shall be brought to pass the saying that is written, Death is swallowed up in victory. O death, where is thy sting? O grave, where is thy victory? The sting of death is sin; and the strength of sin is the law. But thanks be to God, which giveth us the victory through our Lord Jesus Christ" (1 Corinthians 15:51-57). "Then cometh the end, when he shall have delivered up the kingdom to God, even the Father; when he shall have put down all rule, and all authority and power. For he must reign, till he hath put all enemies under his feet. The last enemy, that shall be destroyed is death" (1 Corinthians 15:24-27).

Rejoice, my soul, in view of that glorious day, when thy salvation will be consummated! Never lose sight of it; but steadily look for the coming of thy Lord, that thou mayest receive from him a crown of righteousness.

Prayer

Almighty God, Sovereign of the universe, thou reignest over this world, with infinite wisdom and justice. Darkness, disorder, and confusion surround me; but I am sustained by thy word. Light will be brought out of this darkness, and order out of this confusion. Thou hast appointed a day in which thou wilt judge the world in righteousness, by thy Son Jesus Christ, whom thou hast appointed universal Judge; of which thou hast given assurance unto all men, by his resurrection from the dead. I believe and rejoice in the truth. I rejoice that my Redeemer is thus exalted, and that he will arraign both his friends and his enemies before his judgment--seat, from which he will pronounce the sentence of life on the one, and the sentence of death on the other. I rejoice in the belief of thy word; and pray that my faith in it may become stronger and stronger. Afford me grace, I beseech thee, to live daily under the influence of this great and interesting truth. May I constantly act in reference to the coming judgment. Grant that the future appearing of the Lord may be the joy of my heart, and that when I shall see him in that day I may triumph in his grace, and receive from his hands a crown of life. All this, I ask in his name. Amen.

MEDITATION 16

THE LOVE OF CHRIST

The love of Christ, how peerless and wonderful! How it beams in amazing splendor from his cross, and sheds a glorious light on all that preceded, and on all that followed it! Love was the spring of all that he did and suffered for us!

Did he undertake the redemption of our fallen race? Love prompted the infinite condescension. Did he empty himself of his glory, take the form of a servant, and appear in the fashion and likeness of a man? Love disposed him to submit to the profound humiliation. Why did he subject himself to the law, and obey all its requisitions? Why did he live in obscurity and poverty? Why did he encounter opposition, slander, and reviling from wicked men? Because he loved us. It was love for us that led him to the garden, where he agonized, and sweat as it were, great drops of blood, and offered up that mysterious prayer: "O my Father, if it be possible, let this cup pass from me. Nevertheless, not as I will, but as thou wilt" (Matthew 26:39).

He is betrayed with the kiss of a disciple; he is bound by the soldiers, and rudely led to the palace of the high priest. There he is treated with the utmost indignity, and condemned to death. Then he is hurried to Pilate's bar, and accused of treason and blasphemy, and his crucifixion demanded. Pilate cowardly yields to the clamorous demands of the Jews, against his own convictions. He is condemned, scourged, crowned with thorns, and cruelly mocked. He bears it all with the utmost patience; and suffers his blessed body to be nailed to the cross, and put to death. Ah! Had he not loved us, he would have hurled Pilate from his judgment seat, and laid all his enemies prostrate and lifeless on the ground; and the scene that occurred on Calvary, would never have been witnessed, nor would that doleful cry have been heard, "My God, my God, why hast thou forsaken me?"

The love of Christ was perfectly *free*. He was under no obligations to interpose in behalf of our fallen race. He might have left us to sink forever under condemnation and in deserved misery, without tarnishing his glory. Nor did he stand in any need of our services; for, *with a word*, he could have called into existence a thousand worlds, and peopled them with superior intelligent creatures, who would have rendered cheerful obedience to his high commands. His love, then, was *perfectly free*.

It was as *sovereign* as it was free. The fallen angels belonged to an order of beings superior to our race. But the Son of God did not love them. He did not undertake to save them from sin and misery. He left them to suffer the bitter consequences of their unprovoked and ungrateful rebellion, in chains of darkness unto the judgment of the great day. This superior order of creatures he passed by, without visiting them with the overflowings of his mercy; and, in the exercise of his adorable sovereignty, he was pleased to set his love on our inferior race, and deliver us from richly merited misery!

And how *costly to himself* was the Redeemer's love! Our redemption could not be effected by a mere proclamation of divine amnesty, by merely blotting out our sins. Nor could an incarnate angel, acting and suffering as our substitute, have achieved the mighty work. Infinitely more than this was demanded. The redemption of our fallen race required the interposition and sufferings of an incarnate God. Blood divine, offended justice called for. And so infinite was the love of the Son of God to us, that he willingly consented to meet and satisfy all the demands of law and justice; to yield the obedience which we were unable to yield, and to suffer the punishment which we could not endure.

To form some conception how costly was thy Savior's love, think, my soul, of his lowly birth, of his sorrowful life, of his numberless enemies, of Pilate's judgment seat, of Herod and his soldiers, of the malignant Jewish priests and rulers; and especially of his wonderful agony in the garden, and of what he endured during the three hours of darkness, when hanging on the cross, his Father forsook him, bruised him, and made his soul an offering for sin.

Having considered how free, and sovereign, and costly the love of Christ was, let me now contemplate the rich benefits it confers on its objects. How inestimable, how surpassing all comprehension! Guilty, their guilt is taken away, and all their sins are freely and fully forgiven. Dead in sin, they are quickened to a new, spiritual, holy, and divine life. At enmity with God, they are reconciled to God and brought into a state of favor. Condemned, they are justified and made righteous, through the imputed righteousness of Christ. From the family of Satan, they are taken, and adopted into the family of the Most High, and enrolled among his children. Heirs of wrath, they are constituted heirs of heaven. The Spirit is sent down from above to dwell forever in their hearts, as their teacher and guide, as their sanctifier and comforter, as a pledge of joys to come, and to seal them unto the day of redemption. They are partially sanctified here, and they will be perfectly sanctified hereafter.

They open the book of God, and what do they read? That God has made with them an everlasting covenant, confirmed by the blood of his Son, and sealed to them, at the table of their Lord, with the symbols of his broken body and shed blood; a covenant comprehending time and eternity, and blessings that transcend their highest conceptions; a covenant including exceeding great and precious promises; in which it is written, "For the LORD GOD is a sun and shield; the LORD will give grace and glory: no good things will he withhold from them that walk uprightly" (Psalm 84:11). "He that spared not his own Son, but delivered him up for us all, how shall he not with him also freely give us all things" (Romans 8:32). "Be thou faithful unto death, and I will give thee a crown of life" (Revelation 2:10). "To him that overcometh will I grant to sit with me on my throne, even as I also overcame, and am set down with my Father on his throne" (Revelation 3:21). What amazing promises these!

Contemplating the love of Christ, so rich in its benefits to them, well may the redeemed exclaim with John; "Behold, what manner of love the Father hath bestowed on us, that we should be called the sons of God: therefore the world knoweth us not, because it knew him not. Beloved, now are we the sons of God, and it doth not yet appear, what we shall be: but we know that, when he shall appear, we shall be like him; for we shall see him as he is" (1 John 3:1-2).

For love so free and sovereign, so costly and rich, what shall I render to my Lord and Master? I have nothing to give him, but my worthless heart. Will he accept this poor return? He will; for this is all he seeks. O! Then, let me love him with all my heart, and soul, and might, and strength. Let my heart overflow with gratitude, for his amazing grace and blessings. Let me forever speak his praise; and, as "to this end Christ died, and rose, and revived, that he might be Lord both of the dead and living" (Romans 14:9); let me acknowledge him to be my Lord, and yield to him a cheerful, unreserved, and growing obedience to all his commandments. This is the only way to prove my love to him, who loved me and gave himself for me; for he has said, "If ye love me, keep my commandments:" and again, "He that hath my commandments, and keepeth them, he it is that loveth me: and he that loveth me shall be loved of my Father, and I will love him, and will manifest myself to him" (John 14:15, 21).

PRAYER

Blessed Redeemer, I bless thee for love so free, so sovereign, so costly to thyself, but so rich in benefits to men. May I love to contemplate thy love that shines so brightly in all that thou wast pleased to undertake to accomplish for us, and in all that thou didst do and suffer. And blessed be thy name, that we are sure that the same love still dwells in thy heart, and that in the last day it will appear in all its overflowing fullness. May I make a suitable return of gratitude and love. Take entire possession of my heart, and reign over all my affections and powers, and draw them forth to thyself by the constraining influence of thy Holy Spirit.

God and Father of our Lord Jesus Christ, of whom the whole family in heaven and earth is named, grant me, according to the riches of thy glory, to be strengthened with might by thy Spirit in the inner man; that Christ may dwell in my heart by faith; that I, being rooted and grounded in love, may be able to comprehend with all saints, what is the breadth, and depth, and length, and height; and to know the love of Christ, which passeth knowledge, that I may be filled with all the fullness of God. Now unto thee who art able to do exceeding abundantly above all that I ask or think, according to the power that worketh in thy saints; unto thee be glory in the Church, by Christ Jesus, throughout all ages, world without end. Amen (Ephesians 3:14-21).

MEDITATION 17

SELF-EXAMINATION

I have contemplated the cross of my Redeemer, and meditated on the great truths connected with it; and by so doing I have remembered him, in accordance with the end of that ordinance, for which I am endeavoring to make preparation. It now behooves me to attend to a particular duty prescribed in the institution: "But let a man examine himself, and so let him eat of that bread, and drink of that cup" (1 Corinthians 11:28). The duty doubtless means that he should, by the due performance of it, ascertain his right to a seat at the sacred table.

PRAYER

O thou omniscient and heart searching God, I am about entering on a most important duty; to inquire into, and determine, my real character and condition, in thy sight. I need thine aid; and I beseech thee to compose and to enlighten my mind. Graciously grant the aids of thy Holy Spirit to bear witness with my spirit, that I am thy child, renewed and sanctified by thy grace. Let me not deceive myself with a name to live, if I be dead. Undeceive me, if I be deceived. But, if I am a renewed creature, help me to ascertain and determine the fact, that I may rejoice in my filial relation to thee, my God. Hear me, for Christ's sake. Amen.

The first question, then, which I have to propose to myself is this: "Am I a Christian?" True, I was descended from Christian parents, born in the visible church, and baptized when an infant, in the name of the sacred Three. But, while I should be grateful for the privilege connected with my birth, and duly appreciate my infant dedication to God, in the rite of baptism, I must remember that neither my birth nor my baptism will entitle me to a seat at the Lord's table. The question proposed, imports much more than these outward privileges. To be a Christian is to be born again, regenerated by the Holy Spirit, and united to Jesus Christ by a true and living faith. Am I a Christian in this sense of the name? Certainly I was not born such. I came into the world with the same depraved nature which others inherited; a child of wrath even as they.

Was I ever convinced of this lamentable fact? Were my eyes opened by the Spirit, to see my sinful and lost condition, as dead in sin, and condemned by the divine law to everlasting misery? Trembling under the painful conviction, did I strive, by sorrow and reformation, to flee from the wrath to come? Have I seen the futility of my own endeavors and works to recommend me to God, and save my soul? Do I understand the provision made in the gospel for the gratuitous justification of sinners? Has my mind been enlightened to see the fullness, the suitableness, and all-sufficiency of Jesus Christ as a Savior? Do I believe that he is both able and willing to save all that will come to him? And, under this belief, did I apply to him for his salvation? Do I rely on his merits for acceptance with God? Have I taken him to be my Redeemer, and committed my soul; and my eternal interests, into his hands, and devoted myself to his service?

Have I experienced a change in my nature, and been quickened into a new spiritual life? Have old things passed away, and all things become new? Are my views, feelings, and affections changed? Have I new views of God, of his law, of myself, of sin, of duty, and of Christ? Do I see the comparative emptiness of worldly things, and the infinite value of heavenly and eternal things? Has the current of my affections been changed? Have they been turned from earth to heaven? From the creature to the Creator? Do I love things which I formerly hated, and hate things which I formerly loved? Is sin hateful to me, not only on account of its injurious consequences, but on account of its vile and odious nature, as a breach of the divine law, and as being offensive to God? Is holiness truly lovely in my sight, and do I hunger and thirst after righteousness? Do I love the inspired volume, and make it the man of my counsel and my delight? Do I always pray for the teachings of the Holy Spirit whenever I read it, saying with David, "Open thou mine eyes, that I may behold wondrous things out of thy law?" Has God condescended to hear my prayers? And do I, at times, enjoy communion with him in that exercise? Do I love to pray, and find that I cannot live without prayer?

Has my conduct undergone a great change? Have I a new and a different end in life? Is it the glory of God? Am I watchful over my actions, guarding against temptation and sin? Am I, in a good degree, successful in my endeavors to do the will of God? Do I indulge myself in no sin, and allow myself to live in the omission of no known duty? Is it my sincere desire and prayer to God to be sanctified in my whole nature? Do I take pleasure in the expectation, that hereafter I shall be freed from all sin, and made perfectly holy in the Divine image? Do I desire heaven, not merely as a refuge from evil, and as a place of happiness, but as a place where holiness reigns, and from which all sin is forever banished?

If I can answer these questions *affirmatively*, I may regard myself as a CHRISTIAN.

An advanced believer finds but little difficulty in deciding his claim to the Christian character. He has become so familiar with the nature of the Spirit's gracious operations on the human soul, and with the marks of regeneration; and, by frequent self-examination, become so well acquainted with himself, that the first question is soon settled. But there is another question that claims his inquiry, which he finds not to be so easy to determine. It is this: Am I a growing Christian?

Some believers advance so sensibly in the divine life, that this too is a question easily determined. But how is it with me? Am I making progress in the Christian life? Let me inquire. A comparison of my attainments at different periods of time, may furnish evidence. When I look back upon the secret workings of my heart, do I find that I have gained victories over certain sins; for example, over pride, vanity, worldly-mindedness, unbelief, self-righteousness? Do I see more clearly my entire dependence on Jesus Christ for righteousness and strength? And do I depend more simply and entirely on him for every thing, willing to give him all the glory of my salvation? Am I more humble? Do I grow in heavenly-mindedness, and in spirituality of mind? What other corruptions of heart are mortified and subdued? Am I more devoted to God? Do I love his glory more? Do I take a more lively interest in the prosperity of the Redeemer's cause? Pray more for it, and do more for its advancement in the world?

By attending to such inquiries, and others of a similar kind, I may determine the second question.

But there is another inquiry that ought to be instituted, in making preparation for profitable communion season. It is my privilege to approach my Lord and Savior at his table, with humble and believing prayer for every thing I need. Let me, then, inquire what sins too much prevail, and in what graces I am most deficient; that I may beseech him to mortify and subdue the one, and increase and strengthen the other. What are those sins? Does pride, or vanity, or ambition, or carnality, or lust, or worldliness, or unbelief, afflict my soul? Let me lament them, whatever they may be, before my Redeemer, and beseech him to crucify them on his cross. In what graces am I deficient? Is it humility, or faith, or heavenly-mindedness, or freedom in speaking on religions subjects, or spirituality of mind, or qualifications for my particular work?

What is my situation in life? What relations claim an interest in my prayers? My wife, my husband, my parents, my children, my brothers, my sisters? What do they need? Let me inquire, that I may remember them, at the table, and present their cases before my gracious Redeemer.

Prayer

Accept, O my God, my thanks for any assistance afforded to me in conducting the examination of myself. May the result to which I have come meet with thy approbation. I pray that the evidences of my being in a gracious state may increase in strength, and the evidence of my growth in grace become clearer and more satisfying. Graciously grant that I may be led to a more intimate acquaintance with myself; that, knowing my wants and necessities, I may present to thee suitable prayers. I ask in the name of Christ. Amen.

MEDITATION 18

PENITENT RECOLLECTION OF SINS — SELF-DEDICATION

"And you hath he quickened, who were dead in trespasses and sins. And were by nature children of wrath, even as others" (Ephesians 2:1, 3). Such is the language of an inspired apostle. Believing it to be inspired, I cannot avoid the belief that I was born in a state of sin and guilt; that my nature was depraved; and that, coming into existence in such a state, and with such a nature, I was, from the commencement of my being, under condemnation.

The truth of this apostolic statement, has been confirmed by my whole life. How early did the sinful bias of my nature begin to appear! Surely, if my nature had been pure and inclined to good, impatience, self-will, and selfishness, would not have so soon marred the innocence of my childhood. The impure fountain could not but discover its impurity. The root of bitterness within of course brought forth corresponding and evil fruit.

Youth succeeded childhood, and gave clearer evidences of my sinful nature. Pride, ambition, hatred, and revenge, presented mournful proofs, that I was a fallen creature. As I advanced in years, sin grew with my growth, and strengthened with my strength. Evil habits became confirmed, and the dominion of wicked passion, established. Instead of following the pious in the straight and narrow path of duty and life, I preferred going with the multitude, in the broad road of sin and destruction. God was not in all my thoughts. His all searching eye was disregarded; and, if I could only hide myself from my fellow creatures, I imagined I might practice evil without detection. Thus I lived without God. I could lie down at night without committing myself to the care and protection of his gracious providence, during the silent watches of the night; and rise up' from my bed in the morning without thanking him for my preservation from harm and evil, during the defenseless state of sleep, and without invoking his blessing on the business of the day. What ingratitude, and thoughtlessness, and folly!

How sadly did I neglect and abuse the privileges vouchsafed to me! The Bible was put into my hands, but I laid it aside; and, instead of reading and studying it, to form an acquaintance with its wonderful contents, I preferred other books, and sometimes books productive of evil impressions. The Sabbath came; but I heeded not its sacred import and design, and suffered its precious hours to pass away without improving them, by performing their appropriate duties. And how many of them were desecrated, by doing what was unlawful to be done on God's holy day! I went to his house, but my heart was not prepared for its solemn worship. How inattentive to the word preached! Where were my eyes and my thoughts? How wandering and irreverent! How often did I dare to indulge a sleepy humor in the sanctuary! And when I rose up to pray, how did I insult infinite Majesty, by turning as it were my back to Him, and worshiping some creature; or even presenting myself as an object of worship! Why was I not consumed for my impiety, as were the sons of Aaron, when they offered strange fire before the Lord? Leviticus 10:1. Amazing forbearance of my God!

How innumerable have been my sins! Every day, and hour, and minute have I offended. The want of love to God was one continued sin, staining with guilt every moment of my life. A creature in a state of enmity with his Creator, how horrible!

In the review of my life I can call to mind particular and great sins, for which I ought especially to humble myself before God. There, at that early day, I committed an act which I knew to be wrong, and which I was careful to conceal from human eyes. Then _____ and then _____. (This may be filled up by the reader for himself.) At such a time I was bent on the commission of a great sin; and although held back by a distinct warning of conscience not to persist in my purpose, yet I did persist, and should have accomplished it, had not God interposed by his providence, and mercifully saved me from contracting such aggravated guilt. O! How often have I sinned against the strivings of the Holy Spirit!

How criminal has been my life! How many years did I live without God, without a saving interest in Christ, and without hope in the world! And all the time I was becoming more and more depraved, more enslaved to the world and Satan, and more averse from God and holiness. Had not God restrained me by his providence and grace; had he left me to the impulse of my native and contracted depravity, to what lengths of iniquity might I not have gone! Impelled by evil desires and wicked passions, I might, in the frenzy of sin, have perpetrated an offence, that would have clouded my reputation, and embittered all my days! Thanks to God for laying restraints on my evil desires and wicked passions.

Now, for all the sins I have committed, attended with such aggravating circumstances, and the great guilt I have contracted, I acknowledge that I deserve to die; and if, at any time before the exercise of repentance and faith, I had been removed from the world, with my sins unpardoned, I must have gone down to eternal perdition.

"But thanks be to God, who, for his great love wherewith he loved me, even when I was dead in sins, hath quickened me together with Christ, and saved me by his grace" (Ephesians 2:4-5). And now pardoned by the blood of my Savior, and justified by his righteousness, I feel that I am accepted of God, and blessed with hope; as really and fully as if, in my own person, I had satisfied his justice for my sins, and fulfilled all the righteous demands of his holy law.

Alas! This is not all that I have to confess. True, since my conversion by divine grace, sin has not reigned over me, as it did formerly. Its dominion has been broken, so that I am enabled to serve my gracious Lord and

Redeemer, with a sincere obedience. Yet how feeble my exertions and imperfect my obedience! How imperfectly is my nature sanctified, and how strong still are the remains of sin within me! Well may I exclaim with the holy apostle, "O wretched man that I am, who shall deliver me from the body of this death" (Romans 7:24). How languid has been my love, how feeble my zeal, how sluggish my exertions in the service of my divine Master! Ah! Had I been more sanctified, how much more should I have done to honor him! What opportunities for doing good that passed away, would have been improved! How would my light have shined forth to God's glory! And what advances in the divine life should I have made! I blush in the review of my Christian life. It becomes me to fall down before God in the dust, and beseech him to forgive my short-comings in duty, the coldness of my love, the languor of my zeal, the feebleness of my exertions, and my many sins; and to quicken me by his Spirit, to cause me to grow rapidly in grace, to inspire me with warmer love and zeal, and to enable me to bring forth more fruit to his glory.

To these penitent recollections of past sins, is to be added the renewal of my covenant engagements. By the sacred elements in the Lord's supper a covenant is to be sealed; and, therefore, as I have already entered into covenant with my God, the Father, Son, and Holy Ghost, it will be proper to recollect this solemn transaction, and to renew it, before I approach the sacred table, that I may be prepared to renew it there, and ratify it with the appointed seals.

PRAYER

O thou holy God, in the review of my life I feel ashamed before thee. Behold, I was conceived in sin, and brought forth in iniquity (Psalm 51:5). Depraved by nature, I was born a child of wrath (Ephesians 2:3). How early was this depravity indicated in my childhood, and what clearer evidence of the mournful truth appeared in my youth! All the workings of sin in my heart, during those early periods of life, were distinctly seen by thy omniscient eye. And, alas! How did I wander from thee and the path of duty, as I advanced in age! Instead of loving thee with all my heart, and delighting in doing thy will, my heart was in a state of enmity with thee, my Creator, Preserver, and Benefactor; and, under the promptings of a heart so wicked, I was living in rebellion against thy sovereign authority, and openly violating thy holy and reasonable commandments. How innumerable have been my transgressions! How many years I lived in this unnatural and wicked way! How my guilt was accumulating, and to what awful danger I was exposing myself!

Merciful God, I thank thee for thy patience and forbearance. I bless thee for the restraints of thy providence and grace, that kept me back from the commission of those great sins, to which my depraved nature prompted me. And I magnify the riches of thy mercy, by which, notwithstanding all my guilt and increasing depravity, notwithstanding my neglect of thy word and of prayer, and my inattention to thy preached gospel, and shameful behavior in thy house, thou wast pleased to lead me to repentance and faith, by the gracious influences of thy Spirit, to forgive all my sins, to justify me freely through the righteousness of thy Son, and to adopt me, once a wandering prodigal, into thy family, as a child and heir of a heavenly kingdom. Oh! Amazing riches of grace! How can I praise thee, O my God, enough for all that thou hast done for me a worthless sinner? Here, take my heart, and make it wholly thine. Reign in and over me forever; and bind my heart to thyself in the most fervent love. All this I ask in the name of Christ. Amen.

SELF-DEDICATION

And now, blessed God, admiring thine infinite condescension, and sensible of my great unworthiness, I come, invited by thee, to renew that covenant, in which I have taken the Father, Son, and Holy Ghost, to be my God and portion forever; and in which I have given myself to thee, as thy rightful property, to be thy obedient servant and loving child, for ever and ever. I engage in this wonderful transaction, relying on thy grace to help me to fulfill my engagements. Grant me, O my God and Father, the aids of thy Spirit, that I may be faithful to my covenant engagements, until death. And to the Father, Son, and Holy Ghost, be eternal praise and glory. Amen.

MEDITATION 19

THE SABBATH MORNING

The morning of the Sabbath has come; the blessed day on which, in addition to the usual religious services, I am to take my seat at the table of my Lord and Savior; to hold communion with him, and his chosen people, by feeding on that spiritual and heavenly repast, which he has provided at so great a price. What a privilege! What an honor! Am I prepared for the feast? It has been my endeavor to make the required preparation, by attending to the prescribed duties. Regarding the supper as an institution of the Lord, I design to partake of it in obedience to his will.

In conformity to its end, I have remembered my Redeemer. Standing at the foot of his cross, I have contemplated the amazing sacrifice offered on it, for the sins of a lost world; and, in its light, beheld the truths that radiate from this great center of the divine system, and of the divine dispensations. The lamentable cause of this astonishing spectacle, exhibited to the universe, has passed in review; the apostasy, ruin, and helplessness of our race. I have contemplated the bright display of God's perfections, his justice, his wisdom, and his love, beaming from the cross.

The infinite and complex person of the Redeemer, embracing both his human and divine nature; so wonderfully adapted to the great work, which no man, nor angel could accomplish, but which he achieved, I have devoutly considered. I have thought of his infinite condescension, in accepting the office of Mediator between God, the offended Sovereign, and man, his rebellious creature, and in anticipating so joyfully the accomplishment of it in the appointed time. I have thought too, of his profound humiliation, in making himself of no reputation, by taking upon him the form of a servant, and being made in the likeness, not of an archangel, but of men; and, in the fashion of a man, humbling himself, so as to become obedient to the law, not only in its preceptive, but penal claims, and suffering even unto death, and, that the most agonizing and disgraceful, the death of the cross.

The purity and perfection of his human nature; his holy and spotless life, beaming with love to God and love to man; accordant with all the requirements of the divine law, and presenting a finished and faultless example to all believers, have been reviewed.

I have dwelt on the sufferings of my Lord, beginning with his birth and terminating only with his life—on their variety, arising from the opposition and malice of so many bitter enemies—on their severity in the manner of his death—and on their unutterable and overwhelming nature, produced by God's wrath against sin, in the garden of Gethsemane, where no human hand was seen to afflict him, and on the cross, during the three hours of preternatural darkness.

I have considered the dreadful, degrading, and destructive evil of sin; manifested in the insult it offers to the infinite Majesty of God, in the violation of his most excellent law; so sadly apparent in the history of man, forsaking the worship of God, giving himself up to the vilest idolatry, and debasing himself by unnatural and beastly crimes; and especially manifested in the sufferings and death of God's own and well beloved Son.

The reality and certainty of the resurrection of my blessed Lord, I have contemplated with joy, as demonstrating his divine character, and proving, with the broad seal of heaven, the perfection of his work: and, with his wondering apostles, I have gazed at him, ascending into heaven; attended with a bright retinue of angels, passing by worlds and systems, with amazing speed, to the highest heavens, and there welcomed to his reward, as the conqueror of sin, and death, and hell.

I have beheld him taking his seat at the right hand of God; invested with universal dominion over all worlds; appointed Head over all things to his church; and worshipped by all the hosts of heaven as their Supreme Lord. I rejoice in his reign.

I have contemplated him as the great High Priest of the church, as our forerunner and advocate; as ever living to intercede with the Father for his people; that all the blessings of this life, and of the life to come, purchased by his death, may be secured to them.

Regarding my Redeemer as the appointed judge both of quick and dead, I have anticipated his second coming to judge the world in righteousness, and to consummate the salvation of his redeemed people.

On the wonderful love of Christ, so free and sovereign, so costly and rich, I have meditated, and seen how it was the spring of all that he did and suffered for his people. It was love that moved him to become our Redeemer; love brought him down from heaven to earth; love carried him through a life of poverty and sorrow, affliction and suffering; and love sustained him in the agony of the garden, and under the overwhelming horrors of the three last hours on the cross. And when he arose from the dead, the same flame of love was burning in his heart. It ascended with him to heaven; and there it burns in his bosom, and will burn forever.

To prepare for a profitable communion season, I have inquired into my right to a seat at the sacred table, by examining my claims to the Christian character, my progress in the divine life and what sins I have to lament before my Lord, and what blessings I ought to seek from his bounty.

I have also endeavored penitently to recollect and confess the sins of my life, to humble myself before God, and to implore his forgiveness, And, moreover, I have renewed that covenant with the Sacred Three, which is to be sealed at the Lord's table.

Thus having endeavored to make due preparation for the table of my Lord, I may, I trust, approach to it, with holy boldness and believing confidence. In obedience to his command I am going to a feast prepared by his love; where he is to feast me with his broken body and shed blood. There he will put *symbolically* into my hands the price he paid for my eternal redemption. With this price in my hands, while feeding on his body broken for me, and his blood shed for me, with what confidence may I implore God to forgive all my sins, and to bestow on me whatever blessings I need! Away unbelief. Let me approach to the sacred table with confident faith; and beseech my Lord to increase my faith, to inflame my love, to enkindle my zeal, to augment my strength; to make me more heavenly and spiritually minded, and in all respects a more exemplary disciple. He has infinite fullness to impart. We are not straitened in him, but in ourselves. O! For a warmer heart, for more expanded desires, for greater hungering and thirsting after righteousness, that I may be filled. His inviting language is, "Eat, O friends; drink, yea, drink abundantly, O beloved" (Song of Solomon 5:1). "Open thy mouth wide, and I will fill it" (Psalm 81:10; cf. John 15:7).

PRAYER

My God, and Father of our Lord Jesus Christ, I have, by meditation and prayer, endeavored to make preparation for a seat at the table of my Redeemer. I have remembered him, by contemplating his original dignity, by considering his infinite condescension and profound humiliation, his holy life, his bitter and overwhelming sufferings, and his shameful death. I have beheld him rising from the dead, ascending into heaven, seating himself at thy right hand, and coming to judge the world, and finish the salvation of his people. I have dwelt on his amazing love, and its wonderful results. O! Pardon, gracious God, the coldness of my heart in meditating on these great and interesting truths. Let them ever dwell in my memory, so as to warm my heart, enkindle my love, and bind me to my Maker's service.

I have endeavored, O Lord, to examine myself agreeably to the direction of the institution, and to renew my covenant with my God; and I humbly hope, that the result of my inquiries is in accordance with truth, that I am in a gracious state, and entitled, through mercy, to a seat at the holy table. O! That my evidences were brighter, so that I might rejoice in assured hope.

But, with all my defects, may I not, blessed God, come with boldness to the holy supper, and expect to meet my Savior, and hold communion with him? Assist me, by thy grace; strengthen my faith; compose my mind; and enable me to perform the appropriate duties, when I shall occupy my seat, and partake of the heavenly banquet. Merciful God, I beseech thee to hear my prayer, forgive my sins, give enlargement to my desires and expectations, and vouchsafe to me and to my fellow communicants, a profitable and delightful communion season. Hear me, O God, I entreat thee, for Jesus' sake. Amen.

Meditation 20

At the Table

Here I am, seated at this sacred table, to hold communion with my fellow disciples, and with my Lord and Savior! What a privilege! What an honor! How thankful should I be for the grace I have received!

I am indeed unworthy of the place I occupy. But my Redeemer bade me come, and take my seat at this heavenly banquet; and, in obedience to his command, I have come to feed upon the bread, and receive the water of life. May he grant to me and my fellow communicants his gracious presence! May he unveil to us his fullness and glory! May we sit under his shadow with great delight, and find his fruit pleasant to our taste! May our views be enlightened, and our exercises sweet, affectionate and heavenly! May we be assisted by the Holy Spirit, in the great duty of remembering our blessed Redeemer, and of renewing our covenant engagements.

The Bread Given

I take this bread, O my Savior, as thy body broken for me; I eat it, as thou hast commanded, in expectation that, by feeding upon it, my soul shall be nourished to eternal life; just as my body is sustained and nourished by the common bread on which I daily feed. Thy blessing makes common bread effectual, in imparting life and strength to my body; and thy blessing can cause this heavenly bread to impart spiritual life to my soul. Grant, then, thy gracious blessing; and make this a communion season indeed. Awaken my desires, increase my faith, and enlarge my expectations.

"Do this in remembrance of me," is thy injunction. I will remember thee, my Redeemer. Thy original dignity as the Son of God, the great I

Am, the true and living God, the second person in the glorious TRINITY, I call to mind; and how, in infinite condescension, thou wast pleased from all eternity to assume the office of Mediator, between offended Majesty and his rebellious creatures; and with what delight thou didst anticipate, in the revolution of ages, to undertake and accomplish the mighty work of our redemption. I behold thee emptying thyself, and laying aside the robes of majesty, assuming the form of a servant, and taking upon thyself the likeness of man; and, being found in the fashion of a man, humbling thyself, and becoming obedient unto death, even the death of the cross.

I look at thy pure, and holy, and heavenly life. I see thee imparting instruction to thy disciples and the people; refuting the false interpretations of the Scribes and Pharisees, and rebuking those unfaithful teachers, who were causing the people to err. I behold thee going about doing good, working most beneficent miracles, healing all manner of diseases; giving eyes to the blind, ears to the deaf, feet to the lame, tongues to the dumb, and raising the dead; and refusing aid to none who sought it in faith. I see that holy, perfect, and finished example of love to God and benevolence to man, which thou didst set, and leave for the imitation of thy followers, till the end of the world.

And, O my Savior, I think of thy sufferings, commencing with thy birth, and ending only with thy life; of thy poverty and humility, of the opposition to thy ministry by perverse men, and thy rejection by the priests and rulers; how thou wast slandered and reviled, stigmatized as a deceiver, as a winebibber and a glutton, a friend of publicans and sinners, as a deceiver, a blasphemer, and as stirring up sedition. I see thee betrayed with the kiss of a traitorous disciple, seized, bound, and rudely led by soldiers to the palace of the high priest, and there arraigned before the council, insulted, derided, condemned to death, smitten with the palms of their hands, and spit upon, and buffeted; and denied by Peter, who a little before had professed inviolable attachment and fidelity! I behold thee at Pilate's bar, accused by the chief priests and elders, the multitude stirred up to demand thy death, and to prefer to thee a robber and a murderer! I hear the sentence of condemnation passed upon thee by the Roman governor, who had previously attested thy innocence. Thou art scourged, and then delivered to be crucified. The whole band of soldiers are gathered together in the common hall to afflict, deride, and torment thee! Thou art stripped of thy garments, and covered with a scarlet robe; and, being crowned with thorns, with a reed put in thy hand, thou art mocked as the king of the Jews! They spit upon thee, and with the reed taken from thy hand, they smite thee on the head!

Having gratified so far their cruel and malignant desires, and put on thy own raiment, they lead thee to mount Calvary for crucifixion.

There what do I see? My Lord and Master, the King of kings, and Lord of lords, nailed to the accursed wood, and then lifted up on the cross, and crucified between two thieves, with the utmost ignominy. They that pass by revile thee, wagging their heads; the chief priests, with the scribes and elders, mock thee! Thy companions in suffering join in deriding thee!

Painful and agonizing as were these sufferings, what were they, O my Redeemer, compared with what thou didst endure in the garden, when thou didst sweat great drops of blood, falling to the ground; and during the three hours of preternatural darkness on the cross, when thy heart was poured out like water, under the hidings of thy Father's face, and the consuming fires of divine justice, exacting from thee the punishment due to the sins of the world! My soul is overwhelmed with the amazing scene; I am lost in the immensity of thy sufferings!

Thus, I remember thee, my Lord and Savior; suffering for my sins, dying that I might live, put to shame that I might be glorified! O! Amazing love! How hateful now my sins, when seen in the light of the cross! I mourn, I grieve, I beg forgiveness. I renounce my sins. Here, my

Lord, I would crucify them on thy cross. Slay them, I beseech thee; purify me from all iniquity, and make me holy, like thyself.

The Cup Given

Of the cup, which has now been given to me, thou, my Savior, hast said, "This cup is the new testament in my blood." I receive it as such; sealing to me the new testament or covenant, which was sealed, confirmed by the shedding of thy blood on the cross. Here therefore, at thy table, I renew my covenant with my God. I take God, the Father, to be my father and reconciled friend; God, the Son, to be my Lord and Savior, my prophet, priest, and king; God, the Holy Ghost, to dwell in my heart, as a fountain of spiritual light and sanctification: this Triune God to be my God and portion, forever. And I surrender myself up to God to be his servant, his disciple and follower, and his affectionate child; always obedient to his will, yielding to the intimations of his will, and the influences of his Spirit. And by these symbols, appointed for the purpose, I seal my engagements to be the Lord's.

Of the bread thou, my Lord, hast said: "This is my body which is broken for you" (1 Corinthians 11:24); and of the cup, "This is my blood, of the new testament, which is shed for many for the remission of sins" (Matthew 26:28). By faith I take the bread as thy body broken for me; and the cup as thy blood shed for the remission of my sins. By these consecrated symbols thou art assuring me, that I have an interest in all thy sufferings, and in thy precious blood of atonement. I accept the all gracious offer, the great salvation which thou hast purchased for me; and I regard these elements as outward signs and seals to me, that I shall, in due time, be put in full possession of all its inestimable and eternal blessings.

And now, blessed God, having renewed the covenant, and having received the price of eternal redemption, I feel emboldened to confess my sins, to implore forgiveness, and all the blessings I need.

I confess my original guilt and depravity, the numberless sins of my life, and my remaining imperfections, and humble myself before thee, my God, on account of them. I lament my pride, ambition, and worldly mindedness. (Here let each one fill up the list for himself.)

Forgive, I beseech thee, for Christ's sake, who shed his blood for me, all these sins. Blot them all out from the book of thy remembrance, and let them not rise up in judgment against me.

And I beseech thee to grant me more grace, and to sanctify my whole nature. Clothe me with humility; make me heavenly minded; inflame my love; enkindle my zeal; impart to me that wisdom which is profitable to direct; render me more exemplary in the discharge of every duty; keep me near to thyself, and let me live in sweet and holy communion with thee. (Here let each offer the petitions suited to his own case.)

Blessed God, I embrace this precious opportunity for praying for my dear companion, my parents, my children, my relatives. (Here each may particularize so as to suit his own case.)

Nor would I forget the church of which I am a member. Bless our pastor, furnish him to his work. Quicken and animate all its members. Render them more devout, more active, and zealous in thy cause. Oh! For a time of revival, an effusion of thy Spirit upon us, that all may share in the heavenly influence, and that sinners may be converted in numbers, and thy great name may be glorified.

Bless the whole church with new life and love, with increasing zeal, activity, and usefulness. Revive religion everywhere. Let thy kingdom come, thy will be done on earth, and the world be filled with thy glory. Reign, blessed Jesus, over all nations; and let Jew and Gentile be gathered into thy church, and thy millennian glory be seen in all the earth. Amen and Amen.

Thou, my Lord and Savior, art risen from the dead; thou hast ascended into heaven; thou art seated on the throne of God; thou hast universal power; thou ever livest to make intercession for thy people; thou wilt come to judge the world in righteousness, and to complete the salvation of thy church. These glorious truths I rejoice to remember; and by calling them to mind, I am assured, that thou canst do for me exceeding abundantly above all that I can ask, desire, or conceive. Amen.

AFTER RETURNING FROM THE COMMUNION

I have returned from the supper of my Lord and Savior; I have again been at the banquet he prepares for his disciples. What has been the result? Were my views clear and satisfactory? My exercises pleasant? Was I enabled to receive the sacred symbols in faith, and to use them for their appropriate purposes?

Did I remember my Redeemer with affectionate feelings, calling to mind his original dignity, his infinite condescension, his profound humiliation, his holy life, his bitter sufferings, and shameful death? Especially did I think of the unutterable agonies he endured in Gethsemane, and on the cross, when his Father hid his face from him, while a preternatural darkness covered the earth? Did my sins then, in the light of the cross, appear great and hateful? And did I wish to crucify them, that they might die? Did the Savior's love appear great and attractive?

And, when I received the cup, did I renew my covenant, and seal it with the sacred symbols?

Had I freedom in confessing my sins, and in presenting supplications for myself and others?

Was the communion sweet and pleasant to my soul? And have I reason to hope, that my attendance on the ordinance was acceptable to my Lord? May I look for a blessing from my participation of the heavenly feast?

If I can render an affirmative answer to these questions, I may well bless and magnify the Lord for his distinguishing grace and love.

But if my views and exercises were not as I could wish they had been; if I did not enjoy the presence of my Redeemer, as I wished: yet, if my preparation for the ordinance was carefully and duly made, I may console myself with the reflection, that my Savior is not confined in his favors to any particular hour; and that he may yet manifest himself to my soul, and cause me to experience the profit of waiting on him in his appointed ordinance. Let me, then, look for his blessing, and the gracious and consoling influence of his Holy Spirit.

PRAYER

The Lord be pleased to accept of my desires and endeavors. Pardon whatever was faulty, and graciously add thy blessing to my attempts to serve and honor thee in thy appointed ordinance, before my fellow men. And to thy name be all the glory. Amen.

MEDITATION 22

THANKSGIVING

This evening it becomes me gratefully to remember the favors and mercies I have received from the hands of my God. This day I have been distinguished, by the great privilege of occupying a seat, with the children of the Most High, at the table of our Lord and Redeemer; and the enjoyment of so signal a blessing, may well lead me to review the numberless favors that have been conferred on me.

So many years ago, I had no existence. The sun was rising and setting; the affairs of men were moving on, and living creatures were rejoicing in the goodness of God; but I had no being, no senses, no capacity, either to behold the light of day, or to participate in the movements of men, or to enjoy the blessings of a kind providence. The time fixed in the purpose of the Creator came, and I received an existence that made me a rational and immortal being, raised in the scale of creation far above all the classes of inferior creatures that inhabit the earth. Guarded by a kind and watchful Providence, I have been carried safely through the periods of infancy and childhood, of youth and mature age, and continue to enjoy my existence to the present time. I have been sick, but the Lord healed me. I was often exposed to danger, but he delivered me. "From the pestilence that walketh in darkness, and the destruction that wasteth at noon day," I have been shielded (Psalm 91:6). A thousand have fallen on my right hand, and ten thousands around me; but I have been protected against the strokes of death. Such favors demand my gratitude.

The care, the affection, and watchfulness of my parents, the means of education, instructors provided for assisting me, and a disposition to avail myself of these favorable circumstances for the culture of my mind, and the acquisition of useful knowledge, claim a grateful remembrance.

In due time, it pleased the wise and benevolent Founder of human families, who, at the beginning, said, "It is not good that the man should be alone; I will make him an help meet for him" (Genesis 2:18), to furnish me with a companion, to share in my sorrows and trials, and to partake of my pleasures and enjoyments. To this hour we have been kindly preserved in the marriage relation; and having lived together for a number of years, we behold ourselves surrounded, in the good providence of our God, by a flock of children, on whom to bestow our affection and care, and to train up in the nurture and admonition of the Lord. They and we have been continued in the enjoyment of life; and have been constantly supplied with a sufficiency to meet our daily wants; with food and raiment, a habitation in which to dwell day and night, and fuel to protect us against the severity of wintry cold. What causes of gratitude are here, and how often and thankfully should I call them to mind, that I may not forget the loving-kindness of the Lord.

But there are richer blessings than these, that call for grateful recollection. The restraints of Divine providence and grace, that held me back from those depths of iniquity, to which my native depravity impelled me; the patience and forbearance exercised towards me, while I was living in thoughtless forgetfulness of my Creator and Benefactor, and indulging my perverse inclinations and sinful propensities, and thus swelling the awful amount of my guilt, and urging on my course in the broad way that leadeth to destruction, should never be forgotten. Ah! Had it pleased God to cut me off at any time in my mad career, how hopeless had been my case, and how multiplied my sorrows! Hell would have been my wretched abode! Blessed be his sparing mercy that prolonged my sinful life, that I might share in his great salvation!

The appointed hour came, and my guilty soul was visited with renewing and saving grace. The light of the Holy Spirit was let into my darkened mind. I became awakened to a sense of the importance of religion. My numerous and aggravated sins were brought to view. I saw my guilt, and trembled. "What shall I do to be saved?" was my earnest inquiry. How shall I escape deserved punishment? Like other sinners in their ignorance, I had recourse to my prayers, to my resolutions and reformation. But they were unavailing; the disease was too deep and radical to be removed by such inefficient prescriptions. I found no relief; my disease became more aggravated, and my danger greater and more alarming. Hope fled; despair approached. But, in this extremity, when experience had taught me my own weakness and helplessness, and how vain it was to depend upon my own exertions and resolutions, my Deliverer appeared. The Holy Spirit shone on the word, and in my mind. I discovered the plan of free salvation; I saw my Savior, his atoning blood, and justifying righteousness; and receiving renewing grace, I was enabled to believe in him, and to rely on his merits and intercession for acceptance with God and for eternal life. Justified freely by grace, my sins were all forgiven, and I could rejoice in God.

What a change! I was an enemy to God, but now I am his friend; condemned, but now pardoned; a child of the devil, but now a child of God; an heir of hell, but now an heir of heaven; posting on in the road to ruin, but now walking in the path that leads to everlasting happiness. Amazing change, produced by the quickening and renewing grace of the Holy Spirit! To God be all the glory. I deserve no part of the praise. Had I been left to myself, I should have remained in all the guilt and misery of my natural state, and gone on from bad to worse, and, from day to day, treasured up to myself wrath against the day of wrath, and revelation of the righteous judgment of God. Oh! What gratitude I owe to the Father, to the Son, and to the Holy Ghost, for what has been done for me by his free and sovereign grace; and for making me to differ so much from those of my fellow-creatures who are left to themselves, and do not participate in these inestimable blessings! All glory to God!

Nor is this all that I have to recall to mind of the distinguishing grace and loving-kindness of God to me, unworthy sinner that I am. By his grace I have been preserved in that blessed state of acceptance and friendship with him, into which I have been introduced, by faith in his Son, our Mediator. Hitherto he has kept me from falling into a state of condemnation; as it is written, "There is therefore now no condemnation to them that are in Christ Jesus, who walk not after the flesh, but after the Spirit" (Romans 8:1). If at any time, I have declined, or backslidden in religion, he has graciously brought me back to his service, and revived me.

And this day, I have been indulged with the privilege of partaking of that rich banquet, which the love of his Son has provided for his disciples, and of renewing with him "an everlasting covenant, ordered in all things and· sure; which is all my salvation and desire" (2 Samuel 23:5).

Such are the blessings, temporal and spiritual, so great, so various, so manifold, so inestimable, which I have to record and remember this day, to the praise of my God. Oh! For a grateful heart, and tongue to praise the Lord!

THANKSGIVING

Great and Almighty God, how infinite thy goodness, and boundless thy mercy! When I review my life, and call to mind what thou hast done for me, what abundant reason do I see for adopting the language of David! "Bless the Lord, O my soul; and all that is within me, bless his holy name. Bless the Lord, O my soul, and forget not all his benefits" (Psalm 103:1-2). They commenced with my existence; they have followed me through life, and have continued to visit me, until the present hour. They are innumerable and very great; fresh every morning and renewed every evening.

For my existence, as a rational and immortal creature, and for my preservation through the dangers of infancy and childhood, I praise thee, O my Creator and Preserver. I bless thee for the restraints of thy providence and grace, by which I was kept from acting out the impulses of my depraved desires and wicked passions. For the exercise of thy patience and forbearance, by which the stroke of offended justice was held back, and my guilty soul was saved from deserved punishment, I magnify thy name. Daily have I been fed and clothed, while I was daily forgetful of that bountiful hand, which supplied all my recurring wants, spread my table with plenty, furnished me with raiment, and provided for me a comfortable dwelling. O bless the Lord, my soul.

For my companion, and for my children, and their preservation, I thank thee, O thou wise and beneficent Founder of families, and kind Benefactor of our race.

O! How kind thou hast been in regard to my spiritual interest! Thou didst put into my hand thy inspired word, supplied me with other means of grace, with the worship of thy house and the preaching of the gospel. And what shall I render unto thee, O thou gracious God, that notwithstanding my ungrateful and sinful neglect of these precious favors, thou wast pleased to call me out of darkness into marvelous light. I magnify thy name for the great and wonderful change thou hast wrought in my character and state. Hast thou not, O merciful God, renewed and sanctified my nature, and united me to the Savior by a living faith? Hast thou not forgiven all my sins and justified me by faith in Christ? Have I not peace with thee? Hast thou not adopted me into thy family? Am I not thy child and an heir of heaven? and may I not rejoice in hope of the glory of God? For these unutterable blessings, I praise and extol thy great name, O my covenant God, and Fountain of all good. Forever be thou glorified by me and all thy creatures. And now to the Father, Son, and Holy Ghost, be all praise, forever and ever. Amen.

Meditation 23

Obligations Assumed

The Lord's supper is fitly called the Eucharist, that is, thanksgiving. Well may we render thanks and praise, for the great privilege of commemorating the death of our Redeemer, and of accepting his purchased blessings, whenever we partake of this ordinance. But another duty of a different kind, though not at all inconsistent with the pleasant one of thanksgiving and praise, is demanded. We are called upon to assume covenant obligations, by recognizing God's right over us, entering into covenant with him, and engaging to keep his commandments, and to live to his glory. And is not this a privilege? Does it not claim my gratitude and praise, that I am permitted to return from my wanderings unto the Fountain of light, of holiness, and of happiness; to bind myself by solemn vows of obedience to my God, with the encouraging hope that he will, for the sake of his own Son, graciously accept of my covenant engagements, and afford me grace to enable me to fulfill them?

I have made, in the ordinance on which I have attended, a solemn recognition, that I am not my own, but belong to Jesus Christ, my Lord, and devoted myself to his service and glory. And what could be more reasonable and proper? Am I not his in every sense? Has he not in me the most unlimited property?

Whence did I derive my existence? Not from myself; nor from my parents, who were only the instruments of bringing me into the world. I owe my existence to Jesus Christ; "For by him were all things created, that are in heaven, and that are in earth, visible and invisible, whether they be thrones, or dominions, or principalities, or powers; all things were created by him, and for him" (Colossians 1:16). He gave me existence. He formed my body, curiously and wonderfully constructed, with its various senses, organs, and limbs. He gave me eyes to see, ears to hear, legs and feet to walk, arms and hands for their appropriate uses, a mouth to receive necessary food and drink, and a tongue to converse with my fellow creatures, and to speak his praise. He created my soul, and endowed it with all its intellectual and moral faculties. I am his, then, by *right of creation*.

By whom has my existence been preserved? My parents watched carefully over me, during my infancy, childhood, and youth; and I have daily eaten the food necessary for the sustentation of my mortal frame, and put on raiment to protect my body against the cold. But vain had been my own care and that of my parents, had it not been for the preserving and protecting guardianship of my Redeemer. Had he willed it, food would have become nauseous, sickness seized my frame, medicine proved unavailing; the pulsations of my heart, and the circulation of blood through my veins, would have ceased; my eyes would have been closed, and my active limbs become motionless, by the cold hand of death. Had he willed it, my existence would have been lost, and my being returned to its original nothingness. "In Him we live, and move, and have our being" (Acts 17:28). I am his by *right of preservation*.

And am I not his by innumerable blessings conferred on me? From infancy to the present hour, he has opened his hand, and supplied, by his rich bounty, my daily and returning wants. He has watched over me by day and by night, and saved me from dangers seen and unseen. He commanded the sun to rise and shine, that my eyes might see the light, and behold the beauties of nature; and to set, that I might gaze at the glories of the firmament above, and praise the Almighty Creator. He, by his wisdom, mingled together, in due proportion, the elements that compose the atmosphere, to render it fit for human respiration, that I might inhale health, and not death. At his command the rain descends to fertilize the earth; the grass grows; the wheat, and the rye, and the various vegetables, on which we subsist; the trees bring forth their various and delightful fruits; and animals are multiplied to furnish men with food, and supply them with raiment to protect and adorn their bodies. In all these diversified operations of his wonder-working providence, I have largely partaken; and my heart has been made glad by his rich and long continued bounties. And must I not feel constrained by gratitude, to acknowledge that I am his?

To these common blessings of providence he has added more special blessings. He gave me birth in a Christian country, in a land of civil and religious liberty. He has put into my hand the Bible, containing a revelation from heaven, that I may read and study it, and understand the wonderful plan of salvation, devised by infinite wisdom. He has instituted the Sabbath, that I may enjoy the rest of one day in seven, and attend, without interruption by the ordinary cares and business of life, to the greater interests of religion. He has thrown open to me the doors of the sanctuary, that I may enter in, and worship with the great congregation. He has given me access to the throne of grace, and bidden me come boldly in his name, that I may obtain every needed blessing. He has opened the way into the holiest of all, and permitted me to approach and converse with infinite Majesty. He has imparted to me the Holy Spirit, as a teacher, advocate, comforter, and witness, to regenerate and sanctify my soul, and to perfect holiness in me. He has bought me with his blood, and wrought out for me a perfect righteousness, that I may appear with acceptance in the eyes of infinite purity.

And am I not his, who has done all this for me; bestowed on me such numberless and rich blessings, who has purchased me as his property, and delivered me from captivity to sin, and death, and hell; and has prepared mansions in his Father's house, that I may dwell with him there, in eternal happiness, and in endless glory? Certainly I am his, who has bestowed on me such unutterable benefits.

By right of creation—by right of preservation—by right of numberless benefactions—by right of redemption—by the quickening and sanctifying influences of his Holy Spirit, and by repeated self-dedications to his service, solemnly acknowledged, and ratified, at the table of my Lord, I belong to Him, who "died, and rose, and revived, that he might be Lord both of the dead and living" (Romans 14:10).

Yes, I have solemnly recognized the right of Jesus Christ; and, in the presence of men, of angels, and of God, I have devoted myself, soul and body, to his service and glory. O! May I never forget the solemn truth, and solemn transaction! May I be enabled to fulfill my covenant engagements! I do not belong to the world. Let me then come out from it, and be separate; and manifest by my life, that I am not governed by the sinful views, and maxims, and principles, that govern unrenewed men, but by those that are set forth in the sacred Scriptures. The servitude of Satan I renounce; therefore I must resist all his temptations, and oppose the interests of his usurped dominion over the world. I am not my own; therefore I may not follow my own sinful inclinations, nor gratify my evil passions, and carnal desires. My flesh and sinful lusts must all be mortified and crucified. My body is to be presented as a living sacrifice, holy, acceptable unto God, a reasonable service; and I am to be transformed by the renewing of my mind, that I may prove what is that good, and acceptable, and perfect will of God (Romans 12:1-2). In a word, I must follow Christ, and be holy as God is holy; and endeavor to shine forth in all the heavenly graces and virtues that pertain to a perfect man in Christ Jesus.

PRAYER

My Lord and my God, I acknowledge thy right to me and over me. I am thine, in every sense of the word. Thine by creation, thine by preservation, thine by thy benefactions, thine by redemption, thine by regeneration, thine by self-dedication. I am not my own, but wholly thine, for time and for eternity. In this I rejoice. O! For grace to remember the glorious truth, and to live according to its controlling influence. Let me never forget it. O! Engrave it on my memory, and in my heart. May I, at all times, and in all circumstances, acknowledge that I am not mine own, but belong to my faithful Lord and Savior, who has bought me with his precious blood, and sanctified me by his Holy Spirit, and constrained me to devote myself soul and body to his service and honor, forever. May I be faithful to my engagements, and always live in such a way as to prove to the world, that I am the servant and friend of my Redeemer. Reign in me, blessed Jesus. Take entire possession of my soul and body; and control all the faculties of the one, and all the members of the other, so as to do thy holy will, and bring glory to thy great name, both here and hereafter. Amen and Amen.

MEDITATION 24

THE CHRISTIAN'S WARFARE

The Christian's life is not one of ease and unmingled pleasure. It is exhibited in scripture, by metaphors that imply self-denial, exertion, and danger. It is compared to a race, to wrestling, to a warfare. The Christian has numerous, powerful, vigilant, and deceitful enemies, with whom he must contend. Let me look at them, and contemplate the warfare in which I have engaged, by becoming a follower of Jesus Christ.

The world in which I live lieth in wickedness. Being in rebellion against God, it is opposed to his cause, and his religion among men. It is of course an enemy to all his friends, and will not fail to attempt to defile the purity of their heart, and to turn them aside from the path of duty. It has various enticing objects to seduce them from the way of God's commandments; riches, honor, and pleasure, by which it controls and holds in bondage all unrenewed men. Let me watch against their seductive influence.

If in the prosecution of regular business, it please God, by his propitious Providence, to grant success to my enterprises and exertions, so as to advance me to the possession of wealth; or if he bestow upon me a large inheritance; I am not to refuse his gifts, but thankfully to enjoy them. But, then, let me beware, lest I indulge inordinate desire and anxious care, either in the pursuit, or in the possession of wealth. "Take heed, and beware of covetousness," is the injunction of my Savior; "for a man's life consisteth not in the abundance of the things which he possesseth" (Luke 12:15). "Godliness with contentment is great gain," says Paul, "for we brought nothing into this world; and it is certain we can carry nothing out. And having food and raiment, let us be therewith content. But they that will be rich fall into temptation and a snare, and into many foolish and hurtful lusts, which drown men in destruction and perdition. For the love of money is the root of all evil: which while some coveted after, they have erred from the faith, and pierced themselves through with many sorrows" (1 Timothy 6:6-10). These instructive lessons, let me never forget. Imprinted on my heart, they will save me from every inordinate desire for wealth, and keep me back from all unjust means in the acquisition of gain; and prompt me to the exercise of that liberality which will lead to such a use of wealth, in the support of the gospel and in the relief of the poor, as becomes the character of a Christian, and will secure the approbation of God.

A good reputation is certainly an object worthy of my desire; for without it I cannot adorn the gospel I profess. But then it must be acquired by a pious life and the practice of Christian virtues. But the honors that the world presents as objects of ambition, and that are to be gained by engaging in party intrigue, and party practices, I should refuse and abhor. And yet, if, in the regular discharge of duty, I should be elevated to a post of honor, or a station of trust, power, and influence, let me regard it as a gift of divine Providence, to increase my means for doing good and promoting religion.

"Wisdom's ways are ways of pleasantness, and all her paths are paths of peace" (Proverbs 3:17). The pleasures of domestic and social life, are not denied to a Christian. I may freely participate in them, under the guidance and restraints of that wisdom that cometh down from above. But there are pleasures in which worldlings delight, which pollute the soul, and excite and increase the power of evil passions. Of these let me beware. The theatre is to be shunned as a school of vice; and the midnight ball regarded as an exercise unbecoming one professing godliness, and corrupting in its influence. I am not to frequent those large and crowded parties, that assemble and break up at such unseasonable hours, and so often interrupt the regular worship of families. Nor am I to imitate those inconsiderate persons, who, by luxurious and expensive entertainments, go beyond their means, and tempt themselves to embezzle the property of others, to enable them to persist in their folly. Over all my amusements, recreations, enjoyments and pleasures, let heavenly wisdom preside, and save me from abusing the gifts of a kind Providence.

But there are greater and more powerful enemies with whom I have to contend. "We," says the apostle, "wrestle not against flesh and blood, but against principalities, against powers, against the rulers of the darkness of this world, against spiritual wickedness in high places" (Ephesians 6:12). What a fearful array! From this passage it appears that fallen angels are so numerous as to be distributed into certain orders of government. At their head stands Satan, once a mighty archangel, but now the great enemy of God's kingdom in this world. He attempted and succeeded in the enterprise of seducing our first parents into sin: and ever since that fatal day, he and his rebellious associates have prosecuted, with untiring diligence and malignant pleasure, the dreadful work of tempting men to sin against God. He reigns over this fallen world, and leads our sinful race captives according to his pleasure. They willingly yield to his seductive temptations, which accord with their sinful lusts and wicked passions. Satan and his associates have studied human nature for many ages; and know, by long experience, how to adapt their temptations to each man's temper and circumstances. Ever watchful, they are ready to apply their influence at the proper juncture; and the most favorable moment, to insure success.

With such enemies, so numerous, so malignant, so artful and cunning, and so watchful and untiring in their work of beguiling and ruining men, thou, O my soul, hast to contend. They are invisible to the eye, but they are real, and the more dangerous on account of their invisibility. Against their devices and snares how carefully oughtest thou to watch and pray!

Alas! They find within me an enemy ever ready to unite in their wicked designs, and deliver me up to their seductive influence. My heart, though quickened into spiritual life, and sanctified by the Holy Spirit, is but imperfectly purified. There is still remaining within me "the old man," sin, to oppose "the new man," a principle of holiness, in all his efforts of obedience; so that I cannot do the good I would. Ah! Were I free from all remains of sins, were I perfectly holy, resistance to the devil's temptations would not be so difficult. How much reason have I to exclaim, with the apostle, "O wretched man that I am! Who shall deliver me from the body of this death? I thank God through Jesus Christ our Lord" (Romans 7:24-25).

But in this great fight with enemies so mighty, so numerous, and so dangerous, let me not be discouraged. God has provided me with a complete armor for the battle. There is the girdle of truth to keep the armor in its place, and the breastplate of righteousness to protect the breast. My feet may be shod with the preparation of the gospel of peace. There is the shield of faith to quench all the fiery darts of the wicked; the helmet, or hope, of salvation to guard the head against deadly strokes; and the sword of the Spirit, which is the word of God, to be wielded in assailing my enemies (Ephesians 6:13-17).

Here is complete armor for my warfare. Let me put it on; and thus armed, let me go forth under the conduct of the great Captain of salvation, to the warfare to which I am called; and, with earnest prayer to Almighty God for grace and strength, let me endeavor to be "strong in the Lord and in the power of his might;" that I may be enabled "to withstand in the evil day, and having done all, to stand" (Ephesians 6:10, 13).

I have looked at my enemies; now let me look at my allies and friends. Here on earth I see the host of God's elect; all engaged in the same warfare, and continually offering up to the glorious Head of the church, the prayer, "Thy kingdom come." In heaven I behold the mighty angels prepared for her and my aid; for, "Are they not all ministering spirits, sent forth to minister for them who shall be heirs of salvation?" (Hebrews 1:14). They are more numerous and more powerful than fallen spirits, and render to the children of God signal aid. "The angel of the LORD encampeth round about them that fear him, and delivereth them" (Psalm 34:1). Terrified by a sight of the Syrian host that compassed the city, both with horses and chariots, "the young man who waited on Elisha exclaimed, Alas, my master! how shall we do? And he answered, Fear not: for they that be with us, are more than they that be with them. And Elisha prayed and said, Lord, I pray thee, open his eyes, that he may see. And the Lord opened the eyes of the young man, and he saw; and behold, the mountain was full of horses and chariots of fire, round about Elisha" (2 Kings 6:15-17). And were my eyes, and the eyes of other Christians opened, as were the eyes of this young man, what discoveries should we make, and how should we rejoice in the heavenly guards God has stationed around us!

And when we consider, that JEHOVAH himself is on our side, surely we are authorized to dismiss every dispiriting fear! The triumphant interrogatories of the apostle Paul, become our lips: "If God be for us who can be against us? He that spared not his own Son, but delivered him up for us all, how shall he not with him also freely give us all things? Who shall lay any thing to the charge of God's elect? God that justifieth? Will he do it? Who is he that condemneth? Christ that died, yea rather, that is risen again, who is even at the right hand of God, who also maketh intercession for us? Will he condemn? Who shall separate us from the love of Christ? Shall tribulation, or distress, or persecution, or famine, or nakedness, or peril, or sword? As it is written, For thy sake we are killed all the day long; we are accounted as sheep for the slaughter. Nay, in all these things we are more than conquerors through him that loved us. For I am persuaded, that neither death, nor life, nor angels, nor principalities, nor powers, nor things present, nor things to come, nor height, nor depth, nor any other creature, shall be able to separate us from the love of God, which is in Christ Jesus" (Romans 8:31-39).

PRAYER

Almighty God, in what a warfare have I engaged, by entering into the service of Jesus Christ thy Son! With what enemies I have to contend! The world meets me, to entice me back from his blessed control. It urges its sinful maxims, customs, practices, and amusements, to turn my feet from his commandments. By its wealth, its honors, and its pleasures, it allures me from duty. By innumerable, cunning, and malignant fallen spirits, I am surrounded; who are constantly watching for opportunities to press upon me their temptations. And alas! My depraved heart is ready to seize the temptation, and to side with my spiritual enemies, that I may be led astray from thy holy precepts.

When I consider my own weakness, and compare myself with the number, power, subtilty, and influence of my enemies, how discouraging the warfare! But blessed be thy name, I am not called to war in my own strength. I may rely on thy almighty aid. Thou hast provided for me a complete armor. O! Help me to put it on; and lead me on to fight under the conduct of the great Captain of salvation. I am not alone in this warfare. I have for my fellow soldiers, all the chosen and redeemed of God on earth, who are sending up prayer to God for themselves and each other. And I am taught by thy word to believe that the holy angels are ministering to my welfare and safety. More are on my side than they that be against me. With such friends and allies, I may, relying on the grace of my God, go on cheerfully in the warfare, and entertain a confident hope of a final and triumphant victory over all my spiritual enemies.

I shall at last tread them all under my feet, and exult forever in the finished salvation of my glorious Redeemer. Into thy hands, O my God, I commit my soul. Preserve me, blameless, unto thy heavenly kingdom, and bestow upon me a crown of life, for Jesus' sake. Amen.

MEDITATION 25

WATCHFULNESS AND DEPENDENCE ON DIVINE ASSISTANCE

When I compare my enemies with my friends and allies, I see the latter exceed in number, and far transcend in power the former; so that I may, in this view of my case, well cheer myself, by repeating the triumphant language of the apostle, recited in the preceding meditation. But guarded as I am by the ministry of holy angels, and protected by the Almighty, I must not forget, that I am here in a state of warfare, and on the field of battle, and that, while in such a state, I am exposed to dangers, which demand unceasing watchfulness, and the vigorous exertion of every power I possess. The commander of a well appointed army, confiding in its valor, may, when he sees the inferiority of his enemy, feel assured of gaining victory in the day of conflict. But were he to suffer himself to be deceived by his confidence, so as to be betrayed into security, and to neglect to post his sentinels around his encampment at night, he would act a most unwise part, and expose his army to surprise, by a midnight assault, and a shameful overthrow.

This duty is forcibly recommended by the consideration of certain cases on record. Several of the ancient saints failed in the exercise of particular graces for which they were eminent. Abraham was distinguished by the strength of his faith; yet he failed in the exercise of faith, in more than one instance, by the story he invented to secure himself from danger, to which he feared he would be exposed, by the beauty of his wife.

Moses is pronounced the meekest man on earth; yet he was so provoked, by the rebellion of the Israelites, that, at Horeb, when he smote the rock, and brought forth a plentiful stream of water, to allay their thirst, he spake unadvisedly with his lips, and failed to honor God; and was, on account of this sin, forbidden to enter the land of promise. (See Psalm 106:33. Numbers 20:10-11.) The failures in duty, of these eminent saints, may teach me a salutary lesson, to be always on the watch.

The cases of Lot and David are awakening and alarming. Lot was certainly a righteous man; he is so styled by Peter (2 Peter 2:7-8); yet shortly after his memorable deliverance from the conflagration of Sodom, into what shameful sins was he betrayed by his two daughters (Genesis 19:30-38)? David passed through many great and severe trials, with honor to himself. But after the Lord had delivered him out of them all, and had firmly established him on the throne of Israel, into what shameful sins did he fall that brought upon him such severe punishment from the hand of God, and called for such deep abasement and anguish of soul!

Look at these cases, O my soul, and tremble. See to what depths of iniquity thou mightest fall, if thou wert not sustained, by the upholding grace of God. How necessary and worthy of thy consideration, the admonitions of the apostle! "Let him that thinketh he standeth, take heed lest he fall" (1 Corinthians 10:12) and again, "Be not high-minded, but fear" (Romans 11:20). Peter, after having led us to the contemplation of the end of the world, adds this caution: "Ye therefore, beloved, seeing ye know these things, beware lest ye also, being led away with the error of the wicked, fall from your own steadfastness" (2 Peter 3:17).

The Lord is true to his promises, and I may, with confidence, rely on their faithfulness; but let me remember I am not authorized to expect their fulfillment to me, unless I use the means appointed for the purpose. The great apostle, who well understood the nature of the promises, and their connection with human exertion, says of himself, "I therefore so run, not as uncertainly; so fight I, not as one that beateth the air: but I keep under my body, and bring it into subjection, lest that by any means, when I have preached to others, I myself should be a castaway" (1 Corinthians 9:26-27). And this important direction he has left on record, "Wherefore seeing we also are compassed about with so great a cloud of witnesses, let us lay aside every weight, and the sin which doth so easily beset us, and let us run with patience the race that is set before us, looking unto Jesus, the author and finisher of our faith; who for the joy that was set before him, endured the cross, despising the shame, and is set down at the right hand of God. For consider him that endured such contradiction of sinners against himself, lest ye be wearied and faint in your minds" (Hebrews 12:1-3).

Watchfulness, in a state of warfare, is a most reasonable duty. How frequent the exhortations to it in the Scriptures! "Watch, therefore: for ye know not what hour your Lord doth come." "Watch and pray, that ye enter not into temptation." "Watch ye, stand fast in the faith, quit you like men, be strong." "Therefore let us not sleep, as do others: but let us watch, and be sober." "But the end of all things is at hand; be ye therefore sober, and watch unto prayer" (Matthew 24:42; 26:41; 1 Corinthians 16:13; 1 Thessalonians 5:6; 1 Peter 4:7).

My soul, remember this important injunction of thy Lord, so often repeated by his inspired apostles. Watch against thy enemies, at all times, and in all places: watch and pray.

Another duty that demands my special attention in this warfare, is, to bear in constant remembrance my own weakness and insufficiency, for this spiritual and dangerous conflict. The Spirit of God, I trust, has quickened me to a new and divine life. But the grace already communicated, is not enough for the preservation, and demands of this life. It is not with me, as it was with Adam. He had received his spiritual life in perfection, and was amply furnished for all his duties and temptations; and nothing was required but watchfulness, and the exercise of his inherent power, to preserve himself in a state of holiness. Not so with me. I cannot live on grace received. My life is hid with Christ in God (Colossians 3:3), and must be sustained by daily supplies of grace from my covenant Head.

With what beauty does the Redeemer illustrate the truth, and with what kindness, enforce the corresponding duty! "I am the true vine, and my Father is the husbandman. Every branch in me that beareth not fruit he taketh away: and every branch that beareth fruit, he purgeth it, that it may bring forth more fruit. Abide in me, and I in you. As the branch cannot bear fruit of itself, except it abide in the vine: no more can ye, except ye abide in me. I am the vine, ye are the branches: he that abideth in me, and I in him, the same bringeth forth much fruit: for without me ye can do nothing. If a man abide not in me, he is cast forth as a branch, and is withered: and men gather them, and cast them into the fire, and they are burned" (John 15:1-6).

On this mystery of the divine life, it becomes me to meditate frequently and seriously; that, by bearing in mind my own weakness, I may seek and derive strength from my Redeemer. Then will my experience accord with that of Paul, and I may adopt his language, and say," When I am weak, then am I strong" (2 Corinthians 12:10). The more I feel my weakness, the more shall I feel the need of help from above; and applying the more frequently by faith and prayer to my Redeemer for supplies of his grace, he will not fail to grant them, and render me strong in the Lord, and in the power of his might.

After the extraordinary visions afforded to this great and highly favored man, there was given to him a thorn in the flesh, the messenger of Satan to buffet him, lest he should be exalted above measure. Thrice he besought the Lord to remove from him this evil, which he feared would be a serious impediment to his usefulness in preaching the gospel. It was not removed; yet his prayer was heard and answered to his entire satisfaction. "My grace," said his Master, "is sufficient for thee: for my strength is made perfect in weakness." This divine assurance was sufficient for the apostle, who immediately exclaimed, "most gladly, therefore, will I rather glory in my infirmities, that the power of Christ may rest upon me. Therefore, I take pleasure in infirmities, in reproaches, in necessities, in persecutions, in distresses, for Christ's sake: for when I am weak, then am I strong" (2 Corinthians 12:7-10).

This gracious assurance, let it be remembered, has been left on record, for my benefit, and that of all believing Christians. What the Redeemer said to Paul, he says to us: "My grace is sufficient for thee: for my strength is made perfect in weakness." His divine power can be illustrated in my weakness, as well as it was in that of Paul. Had I the faith of this holy man, I might, as he did, take pleasure in my infirmities, that my Redeemer might be honored, by the sustaining influence of his grace.

Meditation, then, on my own weakness, that I may keep it in constant remembrance, will have no tendency to discourage me; provided I consider it in connection with the all-sufficiency of my Redeemer. He can strengthen me in my weakness, so as to prepare me for every trial and duty. "For it pleased the Father, that in him should all fullness dwell; and in him dwelleth all the fullness of the Godhead bodily" (Colossians 1:19; 2:9). "And of his fullness," says John, "have all we received, and grace for grace" (John 1:16). Here is a fountain of grace ever full and overflowing. At this fountain drank all the pious who lived before the Savior's advent, and all who have lived since that period; and to this inexhaustible fountain may I apply, from day to day, as long as I live, and draw all needful supplies of grace, strength and consolation. Here, then, is ample encouragement to go on my way rejoicing; confiding in the promise, "God is faithful, who will not suffer you to be tempted above that ye are able to bear; but will with the temptation also make a way to escape, that ye may be able to bear it" (1 Corinthians 10:13).

PRAYER

Almighty and merciful God, grant me grace, that I may ever attend to the great duty of Christian watchfulness. May I always bear in mind my own weakness, and insufficiency for the conflict in which I am called to engage, by following my Lord and Master. Never suffer me, I beseech thee, by forgetting my weakness, to become secure, and lay myself open to surprise. May I always be awake to a sense of danger; remembering that it is only while I watch, and pray, and exert myself, I am authorized to expect promised aid.

Let me profit by the recorded instances of failure in duty, by eminent saints; and take a salutary alarm, when I reflect on the sad and disgraceful falls of David, and Peter, and others. I cannot live on grace received. I need a daily and constant supply from my covenant Head, Jesus Christ, our Redeemer.

But, O Lord, I know that while I cherish a due sense of my own weakness and dependence, I have no ground for despondency or discouragement. Thou art Almighty, and able to strengthen me with all might, by thy Spirit, in the inner man. Thou hast promised, that we shall not be tempted above that we are able to bear; and that, with the temptation, a way to escape shall be made, that we may be able to bear it. On thy gracious promise, I desire to rely; and to place myself under the shadow of thy protecting wings.

May the assurance of the Savior, "My grace is sufficient for thee; for my strength is made perfect in weakness," be engraven on my memory and heart, that I may continually rely upon his promised grace and assistance. O! For the faith of the apostle, to be enabled, like him, to glory in my infirmities, that the power of Christ may rest upon me; and find, in my happy experience, "When I am weak, then am I strong."

Preserve me, O my God, safe unto the end. Give me the victory over all my spiritual foes, that I may, at last, enter into thy heavenly kingdom, and rest from all my toils and conflicts. Hear me, O Lord, for Christ's sake. Amen.

MEDITATION 26

THE CHRISTIAN'S REWARD

Reward! What reward do I deserve, for any service I have rendered to my Lord and Master? Ah! had I received my deserts, I should, at this moment, have been a castaway; shut up in the prison of despair, and groaning under the weight of a punishment just, severe and endless. But God had mercy on me, and was pleased to make me partaker of an interest in the righteousness of Jesus Christ.

Jesus is the author of my salvation. He has purchased, by his death and obedience, all the blessings I have received, and shall receive. How explicit the language of sacred Scripture on this subject! "The gift of God is eternal life through Jesus Christ our Lord" (Romans 6:23). "He that heareth my words, and believeth on him that sent me, hath everlasting life, and shall not come into condemnation; but is passed from death unto life" (John 5:24). There is, therefore, now no condemnation to them that are in Christ Jesus, who walk not after the flesh, but after the spirit" (Romans 8:1); "who was delivered for our offences, and was raised again for our justification" (Romans 4:25). "I give unto them eternal life; and they shall never perish, neither shall any pluck them out of my hand" (John 10:17). "But after that the kindness and love of God our Savior toward man appeared, not by works of righteousness which we have done, but according to his mercy he saved us, by the washing of regeneration, and the renewing of the Holy Ghost; which he shed on us abundantly through Jesus Christ our Savior; that being justified by his grace, we should be made heirs, according to the hope of eternal life" (Titus 3:4-7). "But where sin abounded, grace did much more abound, that as sin hath reigned unto death, even so might grace reign through righteousness unto. eternal life, by Jesus Christ our Lord" (Romans 5:20-21).

So plainly am I taught, that I am indebted to the merits of my Redeemer for eternal life, and every other blessing of salvation. All the glory, then, belongs to him; and hence it is, I have access to the throne of grace through him, and am directed to offer all my prayers in his name.

And yet the infinite wisdom of God has established a connection between my obedience to his law, and my salvation. Good works are necessary to salvation, though destitute of any merit; and for the encouragement of Christians, and to quicken and animate their zeal, God has been pleased to present their future happiness in the light of a reward. It is written, "who will render to every man according to his deeds; to them who by patient continuance in well doing seek for glory and honor, and immortality, eternal life" (Romans 2:6-7). "For God is not unrighteous to forget your work and labor of love, which ye have showed toward His name, in that ye have ministered to the saints, and do minister. And we desire that every one of you do show the same diligence to the full assurance of hope unto the end: that ye be not slothful, but followers of them who through faith and patience inherit the promises" (Hebrews 6:10-11). "He that soweth sparingly, shall reap also sparingly; and he that soweth bountifully, shall reap also bountifully" (2 Corinthians 9:6). "And they that be wise shall shine as the brightness of the firmament; and they that turn many to righteousness, as the stars for ever and ever" (Daniel 12:3).

While, therefore, I am permitted to contemplate my future happiness as a reward of my obedience, let me never forget the true connection between them; that the reward for which I may look, is a reward of grace, bestowed for the sake of Jesus Christ; to whom I owe all my present privileges and hopes; and to whose merits I shall hereafter owe my admission into heaven, my acquittal in the day of judgment, and the bestowment of eternal life.

Thus instructed, contemplate, my soul, the glorious reward of

Christians. How bright, how brilliant, how transcendent! Gaze at it; and let it awaken thy ambition, and captivate all thy desires, and throw into the shade all those inferior objects of this world, that would dispute for the supremacy of thy heart.

What will be thy reward? "Be thou faithful unto death, and I will give thee a *crown of life*," is the promise of thy Redeemer (Revelation 2:10). Not a crown of gold, studded with jewels, and brilliant with diamonds, such as adorn the heads of earthly monarchs. These are not crowns of life. They pass from head to head, and will at last be lost in the final conflagration of the world. A crown of life is inconceivably more valuable than the richest crown that ever decked a mortal's brow. It will never fade; it will increase in brilliancy with the lapse of ages. No cares, no anxieties will it produce in my breast. Secured to me by the immutable promise of God, it will fill my soul with unutterable peace and joy. It can never be lost; it will through eternal ages adorn my brow.

Again, I read another promise of my Redeemer: "He that overcometh, the same shall be clothed in white raiment; and I will not blot out his name out of the book of life, but I will confess his name before my Father, and before his angels" (Revelation 3:5). What a delightful promise! Here my garments are soiled and blackened by sin; but hereafter they will be washed in the blood of the Lamb, made white, and kept white, and free from every stain. I shall be perfectly freed from sin, and shine forever in the beauties of holiness. My name, now recorded in the book of life, will never be erased, but remain written there forever. And in the day of judgment, when the universe shall be assembled, my worthless name will be confessed before the eternal Father, and before his holy angels. The Lord of glory will acknowledge me as an elect one, redeemed by his blood, sanctified by his Spirit, adopted into his family, and constituted an heir to an eternal inheritance! What honor! what blessedness!

To raise my hope still higher, the Redeemer utters another promise:

"To him that overcometh will I grant to sit with me on my throne, even as I also overcame, and am set down with my Father on his throne" (Revelation 3:21). What a promise! What human mind can comprehend its import? Well might the apostle say, "Beloved, now are we the sons of God, and it doth not yet appear what we shall be" (1 John 3:2), and another, "For we know that the whole creation groaneth and travaileth in pain together until now. And not only they, but ourselves also, which have the first fruits of the Spirit, even we ourselves, groan within ourselves, waiting for the adoption, to wit, the redemption of our body" (Romans 8:22-23).

Compared with the rich, and glorious, and infinite reward that my Redeemer will bestow on my fidelity, what are the objects which the world holds out to tempt my ambition, and entice my heart? Its treasures, compared with eternal treasures in heaven; its honors, compared with the honors which the Judge of the universe will bestow on his faithful followers; its pleasures, polluted and fading, compared with the pure, refined, transporting and enduring pleasures of immortal beings—what are they? The small dust of the balance! A drop to the ocean!

Rise then, my soul, and let a heavenly ambition animate thy desires, and redouble thy exertions, in the service of thy gracious Lord and Master. Seek those things which are above, where Christ Jesus sitteth on the right hand of God. Set thy affections on things above, not on things on the earth (Colossians 3:1-2). In imitation of the holy apostle, "forgetting the things which are behind, and reaching forth unto those things that are before, press toward the mark for the prize of the high calling of God in Christ Jesus" (Philippians 3:13-14).

What, O my soul, are all thy exertions, and labors, and sorrows, and afflictions, and sufferings, to the eternal joy set before thee? Canst thou not say with Paul, "For our light affliction, which is but for a moment, worketh for us a far more exceeding and eternal weight of glory; while we look not at the things which are seen, but at the things which are not seen:

for the things which are seen are temporal; but the things which are not seen are eternal" (2 Corinthians 4:17-18).

Welcome, death, to put me in possession of a crown of life! Welcome, death, to clothe me with white raiment, and secure such glory to my humble name, as will be attached to it by a gracious acknowledgment of it by my Redeemer! Welcome, death, that I may gain a seat on my Savior's throne, and be like him; living and reigning with him in immortal blessedness and endless glory.

PRAYER

Blessed Redeemer, how infinite thy condescension and mercy! I am a poor miserable sinner, destitute of all merit, and deserving eternal banishment from heaven, and eternal confinement in hell. But thou, in infinite love, wast pleased to undertake to deliver me and other sinners of the human race, to atone for our sins, to purchase for us pardon, sanctification, and eternal life. And yet, for our encouragement, and to animate our exertions in doing thy will, thou art pleased to permit us to look at heavenly blessings, in the light of a reward. Thou hast promised to him who is faithful unto death, a crown of life; to clothe him with white raiment, and to confess his name before thy Father, and his holy angels; and that thou wilt grant that he shall sit with thee in thy throne, even as thou didst overcome, and art set down with thy Father in his throne. Amazing promises! Inconceivable happiness and glory!

My gracious Savior, I would look at these promises, and gaze at the wonderful rewards they hold forth, in the light in which thou hast been pleased to present them; to encourage and animate my heart in following and serving thee. But I desire to bear in mind the true connection between my obedience and fidelity, and the promised reward. It is a connection of grace, and not of merit. Never may I forget that all the blessings of the heavenly state were purchased by thy precious blood, and that eternal life will be the gift of God, through thy meritorious obedience.

Grant, O my Redeemer, that I may never lose sight of the truth; and that, while I look for eternal life as a promised reward of my poor services and adherence to thy glorious cause in this sinful world, I may always cherish an affectionate remembrance, that I shall be indebted for a seat in thy kingdom in heaven to *thy infinite merits*.

To God the Father, Son, and Holy Ghost, be all glory, both now and forever. Amen.

MEDITATION 27

THE CHRISTIAN'S JOY

Joy is a delightful passion, or affection of the soul. It belongs to human nature; and is excited by the possession or expectation of some good. The wicked rejoice, when their corn and their wine abound. The bridegroom rejoices over his bride. The merchant rejoices at the arrival of his richly freighted ship; and at the prospect of the success of a gainful enterprise in which he has embarked. By "giving them rain from heaven, and fruitful seasons, God fills the hearts of men with food and gladness" (Acts 14:17).

And have Christians no peculiar reasons for rejoicing? What is the language of sacred Scripture on this subject? "Rejoice in the Lord, O ye righteous; for praise is comely for the upright" (Psalm 33:1). "Rejoice in the Lord, ye righteous; and give thanks at the remembrance of his holiness" (Psalm 97:12). "Finally, my brethren," says Paul, "rejoice in the Lord" (Philippians 3:1). "Rejoice in the Lord *alway*: and again I say, Rejoice" (Philippians 4:4). From these passages and many more that might be quoted, it evidently appears to be both the privilege and the duty of Christians to rejoice, at all times, in all places, and in all circumstances. "My brethren," is the language of James, "count it all joy, when ye fall into divers temptations; knowing this, that the trying of your faith worketh patience" (James 1:1-2). Similar is the language of Paul: "By whom also we have access by faith into this grace wherein we stand, and rejoice in hope of the glory of God. And not only so, but we glory in tribulation also; knowing that tribulation worketh patience; and patience experience; and experience hope; and hope maketh not ashamed; because the love of God is shed abroad in our hearts by the Holy Ghost which is given unto us" (Romans 5:2-5). Peter accords with both apostles: "Wherein ye greatly rejoice, though now for a season, if need be, ye are in heaviness through manifold temptations: that the trial of your faith, being much more precious than of gold that perisheth, though it he tried with fire, might be found unto praise and honor and glory at the appearing of Jesus Christ: whom having not seen, ye love; in whom, though now ye see him not, yet believing, ye rejoice with joy unspeakable and full of glory" (1 Peter 1:6-8).

And does not thy experience, O my soul, accord with these testimonies of inspired writers? Hast thou not tasted the sweet and delightful nature of Christian joy? When thy mind was first enlightened to see the fullness and glory of Jesus Christ, and thou wast enabled to believe in, and to embrace him, as thy Savior, was not thy joy unspeakable and full of glory? And in thy afflictions and trials hast thou not been supported by the joy of faith and hope? Has not religion spread over thee a sweet and blessed serenity of mind? Be thankful for what grace has done for thee. Yet thou hast failed in the exercise of thy privilege, and in the discharge of thy duty in reference to Christian joy. Thou hast not rejoiced in the Lord, as thou oughtest.

Let me review my sources of joy, and see how abundant they are.

1. *The change of my relative state, is one.* Born in sin, I came into the world under sentence of condemnation. It was a fearful state, to live under the wrath of God, hastening on in the broad road to everlasting destruction! Mercy came to my relief. God was pleased to awaken and alarm me, at a sight of my danger. He presented to my eyes the great Redeemer, and wrought faith in my heart. And now I am pardoned, reconciled to God, accepted and adopted into his family, and blest with hope. What a change! How great and joyful.

2. *The change which grace has wrought in my nature is another source of joy.* Defiled by original sin, and destitute of holiness, I was, by nature, at enmity with God. As I grew, up I became more and more depraved, and alienated from my Creator; and had I been left to myself, I should have forever remained the slave of sin, and utterly unfit for heaven. But

thanks to God, he saw me in my woeful condition, and bade me live. He sent his Holy Spirit who quickened me, when I was dead in trespasses and sins. He imparted to me a new and divine life, to love and serve God. The purifying work is begun, by which I am delivered from the bondage and dominion of sin; and it will be carried on, till I shall be entirely free from all sin, and fitted for a residence in heaven. And is not this great change in my moral nature a spring of great joy; one for which I should be exceedingly grateful to the Divine Author?

3. *Another source of joy, is the portion my soul has chosen.* Like that of other men, the world was my portion. In my blindness I pursued after its enticing objects; as if riches, honors, and pleasures, could render me happy. I was destitute of loftier views; I knew of no better portion; till God was pleased to show me my folly, and expose the vanity of earthly things as a portion for an immortal creature. He graciously addressed to me these wonderful words: "Wherefore come out from among them, and be ye separate, saith the Lord, and touch not the unclean thing; and I will receive you, and will be a Father unto you, and ye shall be my sons and daughters, saith the Lord Almighty" (2 Corinthians 6:17-18). Accepting this all gracious offer, I have through grace, taken God the Father, God the Son, and God the Holy Ghost, three Persons in one Godhead, to be my God and portion, forever; ratified by a covenant transaction. What a portion! How infinitely more valuable than the world! "Whom have I in heaven but thee? And there is none upon earth that I desire beside thee. My flesh and my heart faileth: but God is the strength of my heart, and my portion forever" (Psalm 73:25-26).

4. *The Providence of God constitutes a source of much joy.* The world is not under the government of blind chance. "The Lord reigneth; let the earth rejoice; let the multitude of the isles be glad thereof" (Psalm 97:1). How delightful this truth! My affairs are all in the hands of an infinitely wise Being, my covenant God. He knows how to choose for me, far

better than I do; when to afflict, and when to comfort; when to favor me with prosperity, and when to visit me with adversity. I am cheered with the blessed assurance, "And we know that all things work together for good to them that love God, to them who are called according to his purpose" (Romans 8:28). "Many are the afflictions of the righteous: but the Lord delivereth him out of them all" (Psalm 34:19). How consoling the direction! "Trust in the Lord, and do good; so shalt thou dwell in the land, and verily thou shalt be fed. Delight thyself also in the Lord; and he shall give thee the desires of thine heart. Commit thy way unto the Lord; trust also in him; and he shall bring it to pass. And he shall bring forth thy righteousness as the light, and thy judgment as the noon-day. Rest in the Lord, and wait patiently for him; fret not thyself because of him who prospereth in his way, because of the man who bringeth wicked devices to pass. Cease from anger, and forsake wrath; fret not thyself in any wise to do evil. For evil doers shall be cut off: but those that wait upon the Lord, they shall inherit the earth" (Psalm 37:3-9).

5. *The promises of God furnish another plentiful spring of joy.* They are, as Peter says, "exceeding great and precious" (2 Peter 1:4). They meet and cover every circumstance that can occur, make provision for every want, and comprehend every blessing of this life, and of the life to come. How rich and full these promises! "For the Lord God is a sun and shield: the Lord will give grace and glory: no good thing will he withhold from them that walk uprightly" (Psalm 84:11). "Be content with such things as ye have: for he hath said, I will never leave thee, nor forsake thee" (Hebrews 13:5). "But my God shall supply all your need according to his riches in glory by Christ Jesus" (Philippians 4:19). "Be careful for nothing; but, in every thing by prayer and supplication with thanksgiving, let your request be made known unto God. And the peace of God, which passeth all understanding, shall keep your hearts and minds through Christ Jesus" (Philippians 4:6-7). The Bible is full of promises; and should they not

sustain my faith, and awaken my joy? They were given and confirmed, that we who have fled for refuge to lay hold on the hope set before us, might have strong consolation (Hebrews 6:17-18).

6. To all these sources of joy, I must add *my prospects in regard to a future world.* How sublime and glorious! My Savior has gone into heaven, where he reigns in infinite glory; and has promised to come and receive me to himself, that where he is, there I shall be also; rejoicing with spirits of just men made perfect in his presence, and waiting in joyful expectation for the resurrection of my body, to be fashioned like to his most glorious body; and then, after judgment, to dwell and reign with him, in the highest heaven, in perfect happiness and endless glory. Invaluable hope!

What abundant and fruitful sources of joy, are here set before me! A wonderful change has been produced by grace in my relative state; a blessed change has been wrought in my nature by the Holy Spirit; God the Father, Son, and Holy Ghost, has become my reconciled God and covenanted portion; on the care of his providence, I may cast all my burdens, and look to him for wisdom and guidance, support and protection; his promises on which I depend, are exceedingly great and precious; and my hope beyond the grave, is indescribably glorious.

With such sources of joy opened, and to which I may constantly apply, why do I not rejoice more? Let me take a lesson from a man of the world. His heart is set on the object of his pursuit, and he pursues after it with unquenchable desire. He loses it by some misfortune; he is deprived of his wealth, or of his honor. How is he troubled and distressed! He cannot withdraw his thoughts from the dear object which he has lost. He thinks of it by day and by night; and refuses to be comforted.

Now, my soul, if thy thoughts were more turned to the rich sources of joy set before thee, and thy heart were more devoted to heavenly objects, wouldst thou not rejoice more? Endeavor to love more the spiritual blessings bestowed on thee, to give thy heart more unreservedly to thy covenant God, and to prize more highly thy hope of future blessedness; and then thou wilt think more of the wonders which divine grace has wrought for thee, and be enabled to live more in the enjoyment of thy privileges. Thou wilt go on thy way rejoicing, and find the joy of the LORD thy strength (Nehemiah 8:10).

PRAYER

O my God, what abundant reasons thou hast furnished me, for unceasing joy! Thou hast produced a glorious change in my relative state; chargeable with innumerable sins, thou hast pardoned me; condemned, thou hast justified me; in a state of enmity, thou hast reconciled me to thyself; and expelled from thy family, thou hast adopted me; my nature, corrupted and vile by sin, thou hast sanctified, and art fitting for heaven, by the purifying operations of thy Holy Spirit. Thou hast condescended to become the portion of my soul. On the care of thy ever watchful providence, I am permitted to cast myself, and to intrust all my affairs to the disposal of infinite wisdom and mercy. Thy promises are exceedingly rich and precious. And thou hast lighted up in my soul the hope of immortal blessedness. Who should rejoice, if I do not, who have access to such inexhaustible springs of joy? It is my duty to rejoice daily in the Lord. Nothing should extinguish my joy. I should rejoice in adversity, as well as in prosperity; in afflictions, as well as when exempt from them. But I have failed in this delightful duty. Oh! For grace to adopt the prophet's language: "Although the fig tree shall not blossom, neither shall fruit be found in the vine; the labor of the olive shall fail, and the fields shall yield no meat; the flocks shall be cut off from the fold, and there shall be no herd in the stall; yet I will rejoice in the Lord; I will joy in the God of my salvation" (Habakkuk 3:17-18).

Grant me grace, I beseech thee, O God, to enable me to perform this cheering duty; let joy beam continually in my eyes, that those who behold me, may see the blessed and lovely nature of religion; and be induced to come, and taste, and see, that the Lord is good and gracious, and kind to them who hope in his mercy. Let me rejoice always in hope of the glory of God. In the name of Christ thy Son, I pray. Amen.

DEPENDENCE ON THE HOLY SPIRIT

In the economy of man's redemption, the Holy Spirit has been pleased to assume the office of applying the benefits purchased by the Son, to the souls of men, and putting them in possession of his complete salvation. It is his work to enlighten the sinner's darkened mind; for says the Redeemer, "When he is come he will reprove the world of sin, and of righteousness and of judgment. . . He shall glorify me: for he shall receive of mine, and shall show it unto you" (John 16:8, 14). "The natural man receiveth not the things of the Spirit of God; for they are foolishness unto him: neither can he know them, because they are spiritually discerned" (1 Corinthians 2:14).

It is the work of the Spirit to sanctify the soul. We are born of the Spirit (John 3:5). We are saved by the washing of regeneration, the renewing of the Holy Ghost (Titus 3:5). "God hath from the beginning chosen you to salvation, through sanctification of the Spirit and belief of the truth" (2 Thessalonians 2:13). The Holy Spirit teaches us how to pray: "Likewise the Spirit also helpeth our infirmities: for we know not what we should pray for as we ought: but the Spirit itself maketh intercession for us, with groanings which cannot be uttered" (Romans 8:26).

He is the Spirit of adoption, who forms believers to a filial temper, and bears witness with their Spirit that they are the children of God (Romans 8:14-16, Galatians 4:5-6).

He is their strength. The prayer of Paul is, "that he would grant you, according to the riches of his glory, to be strengthened with might by his Spirit in the inner man" (Ephesians 3:16).

In fine, he is the author of every grace. "The fruit of the Spirit is love, joy, peace, long suffering, gentleness, goodness, faith, meekness, temperance" (Galatians 5:22-23).

So we are taught in the Holy Scriptures to believe concerning the office and work of the Holy Spirit. And have I not found the truth verified in my own experience? Is it not owing to his gracious operations on my soul, that I have become a partaker of the great salvation of Jesus Christ?

How dark and ignorant was my mind in regard to spiritual things! I read the word of God, and heard the voice of the living ministry. All was in vain, till the Spirit shed his light upon my mind. Darkness still covered my soul; and I slumbered on, secure and unconcerned about my immortal interests. But when he who commanded the light at first to shine out of darkness, was pleased to shine into my heart, what discoveries were made! I saw my guilt, depravity, and danger. I trembled. Fearfulness took hold on me; I found no rest, till the blessed Spirit was pleased to reveal the Savior in his fullness to me, and let me see how able and willing he was to save every one that came to him. And ever since I have felt my dependence on the Holy Spirit for his illuminating influence. How darkness veils my mind, whenever he withdraws his light! But when he throws his light upon the sacred page, and illuminates my soul, how changed the scene! What wonderful things are seen in the word! With what pleasure do I think of God, and Christ, and heavenly things! How is the mystery of redeeming love unfolded! How plainly is the path to heaven marked out before me! Never forget, my soul, thy need of the illuminating influence of the Holy Spirit, and daily pray for it.

Not less dependent am I on the grace of the Spirit for sanctification. I was dead in sin, destitute of holiness, averse from God, indisposed to holy action, and indeed unable to perform any acts of the kind, till the Holy Spirit entered into my soul and imparted to it spiritual life. At his command, my soul arose from the death of sin. I received from his gracious power ability for holy action. Faith and penitence, love, hope and joy, were wrought in my soul. I could love God and man. My affections were turned from earth to heaven. I delighted in spiritual things, and felt my heart drawn out especially to the household of faith. The yoke of Christ was easy and his burden light. It was a pleasure to yield obedience to the divine commandments. But were the Spirit of life to withdraw his gracious influence, my soul would relapse into the arms of spiritual death. Blessed be God for the assurance, that the Comforter shall abide in us forever (John 14:16). Grieved by our unchristian conduct he may depart, in a measure and for a season. Then the soul languishes, just as the branch begins to fade and wither, when the regular circulation of the vital sap from the vine, is obstructed. Under the suspension of the Spirit's gracious influence, how do all the graces of faith, and love, and joy, and hope, decline!

Before the blessed Spirit taught me how to pray, and helped my infirmities, I could say my prayers; but I could not worship God in spirit and in truth. Under his heavenly influence how sweet is this exercise of the soul! How freely can I approach the throne of grace! How am I emboldened to enter into the holiest of all, and, appearing in the presence of infinite Majesty, pour out the fullness of my heart before him, in the language of praise and thanksgiving, of prayer and supplication! But, when not thus favored, my intercourse with God becomes formal; and I have to complain of coldness, and languor, and dullness, of my want of faith and fervency of desire. Oh! For the spirit and the grace of prayer!

How desirable the witness of the Spirit! He does bear witness with the spirits of believers, that they are the children of God, both in an ordinary and in an extraordinary manner. When he imparts his extraordinary witness, the soul can no more doubt it, than the prophets could doubt that they were inspired. The Spirit is then seen in his own light, just as the sun is in his light. If, my soul, this especial favor has been vouchsafed to thee, thou knowest the meaning of this extraordinary witness of the Holy Spirit; thou hast had experience of the love, and joy, and hope, lighted up by the heavenly vision; thou didst rejoice in the assurance of thy adoption into the family of God, and couldst cry with unfaltering tongue, "Abba, Father."

It is not, however, from this extraordinary witness of the Spirit, that a settled, abiding conviction of being in a gracious state of divine acceptance, is to be obtained. The heavenly vision is soon withdrawn; and may after a while be succeeded by doubts and fears. Such, my soul, thou hast experienced; and thou hast been stirred to diligence in endeavors to make thy calling and election sure. Hast thou, by studying the nature of the Spirit's gracious work, by repeated selfexamination, and earnest prayer for his witness, arrived at a settled belief of having enjoyed his renewing grace, and of being in a state of friendship with God through Jesus Christ? Be thankful for the blessing, and walk with humility and watchfulness, depending on the light and teaching and assistance of the Holy Spirit.

And is he not the strength of my soul? When the Spirit imparts his grace, my faith is strong, my hope bright, and my purpose firm; and, trusting in God, I can go on cheerfully in the path of duty, boldly meet my enemies, and patiently endure trials and afflictions. But how different my experience, when he is pleased in any measure to withdraw his strengthening influence!

Thus, in these various ways, I am taught my entire and constant dependence on the grace of the Holy Spirit. But how slow am I in learning this great truth, so essential to my security and progress in the divine life! Forget it not, my soul; let it be imprinted deeply on thy memory, and keep thee watchful and prayerful. So shall the Comforter dwell in thee forever, and be a fountain of light, of grace, of strength, and of joy; till having finished thy course on earth, thou shalt have arrived at that perfect state of holiness and blessedness, where variations in feelings, depressions of spirits, and doubts and fears, will be unknown; and where thou wilt exult forever in fullness of light, and joy, and glory.

PRAYER

Holy Spirit, one with the Father and the Son, I acknowledge thee to be the author of all spiritual light, and grace, and strength, to my soul. Thou hast assumed the office of applying the purchased salvation of Christ to the children of men, and of preparing them for an eternal residence in heaven. Hast thou not quickened my soul to a divine life? Hast thou not enlightened my dark mind with heavenly light? Hast thou not renewed and sanctified my depraved nature? Hast thou not taught me how to pray? Hast thou not borne witness with my spirit, that I am a child of God? And hast thou not sealed me unto the day of redemption? I thank thee, O gracious Spirit, for these great and signal favors. Dwell in my heart forever. Work there with greater power. Subdue and expel from my soul every depraved lust and sinful desire. Carry on and perfect in me thy blessed work. Cherish within me every Christian grace and virtue. Impress on me the image of my divine Redeemer. Strengthen me with all might in the inner man. Impart to me thy divine consolations. Shed abroad upon my heart the love of God. Let me never grieve thee, but always lay open my soul to thy holy influence, and yield cheerfully and promptly to every suggestion from thee. Perfect thy work in me, and fit me for the enjoyment of that eternal inheritance of the saints in light, for which I hope. Grant me all this, O Holy Spirit, for Christ's sake. Amen.

Meditation 29

Growth in Grace

The law of increase and progress prevails in all the works of the Almighty. He could, if it had been his pleasure, have spoken this world into existence, disposed, arranged, and adorned, just as it was, when the light of the seventh day revealed it to the eyes of our first parents, in all its beauty and glory. But it pleased God to put forth his creating power in a different way. First he brought the chaotic mass into existence; and then disposed of the elements into their various forms, arranged the land and water, formed the lights of heaven, and perfected his plan, by the labors of six days.

The same law rules in Providence. The acorn is planted; from which springs the sapling, which, in the course of years, grows into the majestic oak. Man is at first an infant, then passes through childhood and youth, and at length reaches the full stature of manhood. His mind is gradually developed from its first conception, till it is so expanded as to contain stores of learning and science.

In redemption, the same law is found in operation. Ages rolled away before the Son of God came into the world to achieve his great work of making an atonement for sin, and furnishing us with a righteousness for our justification. Fifteen hundred years were occupied in completing the canon of sacred Scripture.

By the same law is the application of salvation to believing sinners governed. God might, if it had pleased him, have finished the work in a moment, and presented every believer at once perfect in Christ Jesus, in all the beauties of holiness, and in the enjoyment of complete happiness. But infinite wisdom has adopted a different plan. Spiritual life is at first communicated to the soul in an incipient state; and then cherished, and preserved, and increased, till it reaches perfection in glory.

By the grace of God, I have been brought into a state of reconciliation and friendship with him. My sins have all been pardoned, and my person justified, through the imputed righteousness of my blessed Redeemer. My nature has been sanctified by his Holy Spirit, so that a transforming moral change has passed over all the faculties of my soul.

For what grace has wrought for me, I have abundant reason for thanksgiving and praise to God. But great as is the change effected in my nature, and protected as I am against condemnation, through my union to Christ, and participation in his merits by faith, I am by no means to be satisfied with my present attainments in grace. There is room for great improvement. None of my faculties have been perfected. My mind is not freed from darkness, nor is my heart purified from all sin. My love, and faith, and joy, and hope, and holiness, are all imperfect. The old man still remains to struggle with the new man; sin in my members still wars with the law of my mind. In such a state of imperfection, when so much remains to be effected, before I can reach the perfection to which I am destined; it would betray much ignorance of duty, and much ingratitude for what God has wrought for me, were I to rest contented with present attainments, and not labor to reach a more advanced stage in the work of divine grace. While so much sin remains to be mortified within me, and all my graces are so imperfect, how can I rest satisfied? Surely I ought to labor after increased holiness, and growing conformity to the image of Christ.

So acted Paul. He had made great attainments in the divine life; but he did not imagine he had attained to perfection. One thing he did, "forgetting the things that were behind, and reaching forth unto those things which were before, he pressed toward the mark for the prize of the high calling of God in Christ Jesus" (Philippians 3:13-14) and oppressed with the burden of sin, he exclaimed, "O wretched man that I am! who shall deliver me from the body of this death?" (Romans 7:24).

Here is an example worthy of imitation. Let me look at my remaining depravity; and, groaning within myself, let me earnestly desire the Deliverer's hand. Contemplating the great sacrifice for sin, and considering what my Redeemer suffered for my sins, let me abhor them, and strive to crucify them on his cross. I have indeed no reason to believe that I shall ever, in this sinful world, attain to perfect holiness; yet doubtless I ought to be always stimulated in my exertions by so lofty an aim. So glorious is my destiny: and were I to aim at anything lower, I should be unworthy of the prize held forth to view, to inflame my ambition, and to animate my exertions. Laying aside, then, every weight, and removing every obstruction out of the way, let me run the race that is set before me.

The strongest motives urge me to endeavor to grow in grace. Duty calls for it. "Grow in grace," is an apostolic injunction (2 Peter 3:18); "Be ye therefore perfect, even as your Father which is in heaven is perfect" (Matthew 5:48). "But as he which hath called you is holy, so be ye holy in all manner of conversation" (1 Peter 1:15). So plainly is the duty enjoined.

The design of Christ's death demands it. "Looking for that blessed hope, and the glorious appearing of the great God and our Savior, Jesus Christ; who gave himself for us, that he might redeem us from all iniquity, and purify us unto himself a peculiar people, zealous of good works" (Titus 2:13-14). Was this the design of my Redeemer? Did he die, that I might be holy, and finally delivered from all sin? And shall I dare to oppose his blessed design, by indulging in any sin, or by being remiss in my exertions to overcome it in every form? Forbid it, gracious God. Inspire my soul with increasing hatred of all sin, and quicken my efforts to crucify my lusts, and to become daily more and more conformable to thy likeness. May I long for that perfection of nature, to which I am destined; and to put me in possession of which my Savior died.

Ample encouragement is given to animate my exertions, in making greater attainments in the divine life. "And the very God of peace sanctify you wholly; and I pray God your whole spirit, and soul, and body, be preserved blameless unto the coming of our Lord Jesus Christ. Faithful is he that calleth you, who also will do it" (1 Thessalonians 5:23-24). God is faithful to his engagements with his Son; and therefore he will perfect the work of sanctification in all who have been redeemed by his blood, and are united to him by faith. Embrace, then, my soul, this gracious encouragement, that thy exertions will not be in vain, but crowned with complete success. Hunger and thirst after righteousness, and thou shalt be filled.

Consider too the influence which growth in grace will have upon thy future blessedness. Hear the exhortation of the apostle Peter: "Giving all diligence, add to your faith virtue; and to virtue knowledge; and to knowledge temperance; and to temperance patience; and to patience godliness; and to godliness brotherly kindness; and to brotherly kindness charity. For if these things be in you, and abound, they make you that ye shall be neither barren nor unfruitful in the knowledge of our Lord Jesus Christ. But he that lacketh these things is blind, and cannot see afar off, and hath forgotten that he was purged from his old sins. Wherefore the rather, brethren, give diligence to make your calling and election sure: for if ye do these things ye shall never fall: for so an entrance shall be ministered unto you abundantly into the everlasting kingdom of our Lord and Savior Jesus Christ" (2 Peter 1:5-11).

How important, O my soul, is growth in grace to thy present peace, and enjoyment, and usefulness! How plainly and forcibly is it enjoined on thee as a duty! How touchingly is it enforced by a consideration of the design of thy Redeemer's death, who has purchased thee with his precious blood! What encouragement is presented to urge thee on in the glorious career, by the assurance of necessary aid and final success! And how will every step in this heavenly course, influence and augment thy future happiness and glory! Pressed by such motives, wilt thou not put forth every exertion to grow in grace, and to approximate towards a state of perfect holiness; that at last thou mayest be prepared to take thy station, with all the redeemed, around the throne of God, to praise and enjoy him forever and ever?

This, then, be thy high aim. Look to it. Keep thine eyes constantly on it. Pray for the aid of the Holy Spirit, to help thee onward in thy heavenly course; and daily beseech God, that thou mayest grow in grace, and finally reach "the unity of the faith, and of the knowledge of the Son of God, unto a perfect man, unto the measure of the stature of the fullness of Christ" (Ephesians 4:13), and that when he shall appear, thou mayest appear with him in glory, and be like him, and "see him as he is" (Colossians 3:4, 1 John 3:2).

PRAYER

O! Most holy God, the heavens are not clean in thy sight, and thou chargedst thine angels with folly. How, then, must I appear in the sight of infinite purity! By thy free and rich grace, I have been, I trust, renewed, and sanctified, and changed into thy image. But how unlike to thee am I still! My mind is dark; my will rebellious; my affections cleave too much to this earth; my love to thee is cold; my heart is not occupied, as it should be, with heavenly things. How much yet remains to be done, before I can reach that perfection in heart, and in life to which I am destined. Oh! Never suffer me to be satisfied with any attainments that I have made, or shall make, in the present imperfect state of human nature. I pray, that I may ever press on in my career of holiness, and constantly endeavor to grow in grace. Duty calls for it; the design of Christ's death demands it; ample encouragement is given to expect help from on high; the more I grow in grace, the more peace of mind shall I enjoy, and the more useful in life shall I be; and a brighter crown will hereafter encircle my brow, and I shall occupy a higher seat in heaven at last.

O my God, grant that I may ever feel the quickening influence of these great motives; so that, my exertions being stimulated, I may make greater progress in the divine life. Let me never, I beseech thee, O my God, lose sight of the great duty of growing in grace. May I constantly aim at it; and strive to become more and more conformed to thy most holy image. Crown my efforts with success; and, at last, may an abundant entrance into thy everlasting kingdom be ministered unto me, through Jesus Christ, thy Son. "Now unto him that is able to do exceeding abundantly above all that we ask, or think, according to the power that worketh in us; unto him be glory in the church, by Christ Jesus, throughout all ages, world without end. Amen" (Ephesians 3:20-21).

THE END